Iroquois on Fire

Iroquois on Fire

A VOICE FROM THE MOHAWK NATION

Douglas M. George–Kanentiio

Foreword by Vine Deloria

Native America: Yesterday and Today
Bruce E. Johansen, Series Editor

PRAEGER

Westport, Connecticut
London

Library of Congress Cataloging-in-Publication Data

George-Kanentiio, Doug.
Iroquois on fire : a voice from the Mohawk nation / Douglas M.
    George-Kanentiio ; foreword by Vine Deloria.
        p. cm. -- (Native America, ISSN 1552-8022)
    Includes bibliographical references and index.
    ISBN 0-275-98384-6
    1. Mohawk Indians—History. 2. Mohawk Indians—Government
relations. 3. Mohawk Indians—Social life and customs. I. Title.
II. Series: Native America (Praeger Publishers)
E99.M8G46 2006
974.7004'975542—dc22   2006012139

British Library Cataloguing in Publication Data is available.

Library of Congress Catalog Card Number: 2006012139
ISBN: 0–275–98384–6
ISSN: 1552–8022

First published in 2006

Praeger Publishers, 88 Post Road West, Westport, CT 06881
An imprint of Greenwood Publishing Group, Inc.
www.praeger.com

Printed in the United States of America

The paper used in this book complies with the
Permanent Paper Standard issued by the National
Information Standards Organization (Z39.48–1984).

10 9 8 7 6 5 4 3 2 1

Contents

Series Foreword

Akwesasne—"The Land Where the Partridge Drums"—the St. Regis Mohawk reservation on some non-Native maps, is a land of very large contrasts. At the confluence of many rivers, it has some of the most gratifying watercourse scenery anywhere, but don't eat the fish. They're laced with PCBs and other toxins. The soil is rich, but watch what you eat. It's toxic in places, as well. And certainly watch how often you breast-feed your infant. You, and your progeny, are what you eat.

Akwesasne has vibrant family life, and, occasionally, enough smuggling and casual violence to remind one of the Bronx; the same place has become the home of many, varied, small businesses of the legal variety as well.

Akwesasne is also subject to the jurisdiction of a half-dozen governments—imagine living in a neighborhood that is bisected not only by the border between the United States and Canada, but also between Ontario and Quebec. Thus, within a few miles, one can be subject to local (reservation) government sanctioned by Canada and the United States. And that's not all— a traditional Mohawk Council of Chiefs, part of the original, pre-Columbian, Haudenosaunee (Iroquois) Confederacy, is respected widely on both sides of the border.

Anyone wishing to navigate such a place will quickly discover that it has a rich history and many stories to tell. No one except an absolute fool also realizes very quickly that you don't get far at Akwesasne without a guide.

Our guide for this journey is Doug George-Kanentiio, whom I met shortly after the events that you soon will come to know as "the Troubles," in 1990.

An Akwesasne Mohawk, Doug was editing *Akwesasne Notes* and its local counterpart, *Indian Time*, at the time. A number of Mohawks had suggested that I write a book about events in their homeland, which I did (*Life and Death in Mohawk Country*, 1993). My book was an honest attempt, not bad at all for an outsider, Doug once told me. More than once, however, Doug also told me that he would someday write the story in his own, Mohawk words. This book is that story.

I am honored to have played a role in readying for publication this uniquely Mohawk account of an historic time, in an historic place. *Iroquois on Fire* is part of an ongoing series, "Native America: Yesterday and Today," which endeavors to share with general readers new perspectives on the history of the Americas' first human inhabitants, told from perspectives as close as possible to the people who experienced them.

Bruce E. Johansen
Series Editor
Omaha, Nebraska
January 17, 2006

Foreword

A deadly struggle is taking place that has immense importance for Indian tribes today, yet news of the issues and incidents seems to be suppressed. Indeed, since the Cornwall Bridge incident in the 1970s, very little has come out regarding the conflict in New York between the traditional Six Nations people, the assimilated people of Indian descent who have controlled the tribal governments approved by the federal government, the casino operators, the state of New York, and the Department of the Interior. Indeed, there are so many players that it boggles the mind to understand what has been happening.

We do hear occasionally of the gigantic awards given to the tribes of the Six Nations in their land claims against the state of New York, only to be followed by appeals to higher courts, where tortured rhetoric and reasoning deprive the Indians of their hard-won victory. Indeed, if one follows the litigation of the Oneida claim, it is like watching a tennis match, with one of the players having the right to determine for the other the boundary lines of the court. One expects rabbits to be pulled from hats as a case proceeds up the judicial structure, but sometimes the courts are pulling whole herds of cattle and buffalo from nowhere. Judgments often appear to be the first blush of contact between the tribes and their adversaries, and judges and justice are not a bit ashamed of their threadbare reasons for denying the Indian claims.

Edmund Wilson painted a heroic picture of the struggle of the Six Nations to maintain their traditions and culture in his memorable *Apologies to the*

Iroquois many years ago, but today, these apologies, and others issued since, are nothing but smoke—not the religious smoke that moves upward toward the Creator, cleansing the world, but clouds of spiritual pollution. The struggle today involves the perfidy of the United States at the highest levels, and this perfidy involves the virtual destruction of the English language and the resurrection of outmoded concepts, such as laches, that are used to deny the Six Nations from playing on level ground.

At a deeper level, as Doug George-Kanentiio makes clear in this book, we are seeing one of the oldest democracies destroyed by the careless claims of representation made by people part Indian who are motivated, as are most Americans, by greed and lust for power. Today, traditional Iroquois men must carry guns to protect themselves, while other Iroquois, partisans of the casinos, carry weapons to eliminate their opposition. The situation has become desperate because the federal government, in trying to resolve the conflict, has relied on old slogans of government that had no power to convince or cultivate loyalty from the very beginning. It is not convincing for federal officials to ask the rank and file of Iroquois people to accept the dictates of tribal council governments the United States has created or helped to create. That lesson has not been learned in New York or Canada, and it is being soundly rejected in Iraq and Afghanistan.

Everything you want to know—and lots more you don't want to know—is contained in this book. So read about the fire fights. They are well documented here. Read about the manipulation of federal Indian law that has been so severe as to virtually destroy any semblance of rationality, a quality that law must possess as the primary reason for its existence. Read about the hardships of the traditional people as a bevy of government agencies uphold the unfair decisions of puppets and criminals. Could over $700 million in illegal cigarettes have been smuggled across the border by renegade Indians? Yes, it could—and some of them have still not been punished. Could there have been vicious fire fights between gangs of Iroquois, some protecting home and traditions, others fighting for illusory prizes they will never enjoy?

The tale is too fantastic to be believed—could something like this conflict persist year after year, decade after decade, without the public becoming aware of it? Yes, indeed, it could, and it has been happening and will continue to happen. George-Kanentiio tells us in the stark terms of his own life and participation in the conflict that the traditional people will survive in spite of the barriers that have been erected against them. Just a glance at the chronology of the "list of terror" compiled for the short period from March 23, 1990, to April 24, 1990, will reveal the tremendous havoc brought into Iroquois country by the casino operators, suggesting that a choice had been made by the people in power that gaming is more important than people. It does not take much imagination to understand that these conditions—continuing assaults, belittlement of the people's concerns, and attitudes designed only to inflame the situation further—are continuing today. This attitude is directly opposed to the philosophy of the United States Constitution and the religious beliefs of the Six Nations. Yet people in power are given the privilege of defining Indians and Indian rights to suit their fancies.

Is there a solution to total chaos? Of course: the government can, at any time, step into a chaotic situation and assume a trusteeship over the people, lands, and properties of the Six Nations and manage their affairs. Then an accurate census of people entitled to live on the Six Nations reserves could be made, a constitution can be drawn up, and this document could be submitted to the people along with another choice—government by the traditional chiefs. Then there could be monitoring of the governing body of the reserve for several years, ensuring that fair elections and choices become everyday activities, and, finally, a complete release of governing powers to the properly elected people.

In essence, this process is being used in Iraq at great cost to American men and women serving in the armed forces. We are told that other people should have the same democracy that we function under. I do not say "enjoy" because our country is being torn apart under the guise of protecting us from mysterious and unknown terrorists—unless we include Saudi Arabia, which seems to supply a high percentage of people to the various resistance groups in the Middle East. If it can be done in Iraq, why not here? Why allow the destruction of the world's longest surviving democracy to occur under the guise of following obscure and irrelevant federal laws?

What is the lesson for other tribes here? Well, similar circumstances exist in California, as incumbent, self-appointed people purge the rolls of their tribes so they can remain in office. In Minnesota, there is already a substantial challenge lodged against the existing tribal government, and it shows some promise of being upheld. Indian country is just one incident away from complete chaos caused by greedy people wanting power and riches. Other tribes that are abusing their people might well read this book and see into the future.

This book made my blood boil at the injustice being perpetrated on innocent people. I hope it has the same effect on other readers. I think it's time something was done.

Vine Deloria

From the author:

I knew the late Vine Deloria for many years. I had the honor of working with him when we were trustees for the National Museum of the American Indian and as his assistant for the historic "Traditional Knowledge" series he initiated in 1992. He was determined to rewrite North American history by challenging the lies used to obliterate and obscure this land's indigenous peoples and he succeeded through a series of books, articles and speeches which in turn sparked an intellectual, political and spiritual revolution among Native nations which continues to reverberate.

Vine was a contemporary prophet, showing us that the keys to planetary survival were within our ancestral teachings. He was an accomplished scholar who found great comfort and profound wisdom in the oral traditions of his own Lakota Nation. He held in high esteem those Native communities which had bucked the odds and somehow managed to retain a distinct national identity. His Foreword for this book was one of the last things he wrote before passing into the spirit world, a contribution which renews my sense of humility and sharpens my grief for a human being removed from us far too soon.

May he be warmly embraced by those who have gone on before—and may he be there when it is our turn to walk among the stars.

Doug-Kanentiio

CHAPTER 1

Origins

The origins of the Iroquois have been a matter of speculation for anthropologists, historians, and archaeologists. Various theories as to where the Iroquois came from have been suggested, but they are similar in one way: the Iroquois are not from the northeast, having migrated to the region from another place, most likely the southwest.

For the Iroquois, there is no doubt but that their identity as a distinct people took form in the region south of the St. Lawrence River, north of the Susquehanna, and east of the Niagara peninsula. But the ancestors of the Iroquois originated in a place far from what would become their homelands, in an arid area bordered by bare escarpments and hidden valleys.

The origin story for the Iroquois has been an oral tradition carried across hundreds of generations. Those who are entrusted with its details are told of the exodus of a small band of people from the southwestern regions of the North American continent across the Great Plains. The band left the dry lands into buffalo territory before arriving at the western banks of the Mississippi River where it receives the waters of the Missouri and Ohio.

The oral tradition continues, describing the ecological prosperity of the area and the alliance made with a particular nation whom the band referred to as the Wolves, but are now known as the Pawnee. After living along the Mississippi for some time the band traveled in canoes up the Ohio River before splitting into a number of smaller groups. One went southeast across a ridge of mountains, where they became, in time, the Cherokee. Others went east, where they evolved into the Susquehannas or Conestoga Nation. Three factions headed northeast and established homelands in what is now Ontario. They were the Tobacco, Huron (Wyandot), and Neutrals. Another group settled along the eastern shore of Lake Erie. The Erie Nation occupied most of western Pennsylvania. The ancestors of the Wenro Nation elected to remain east of the Niagara River and west of the Genessee.

The main band continued across Lake Ontario and down the St. Lawrence before finally arriving at a place near what is now Quebec City. There they were subdued by a physically smaller but more numerous people called the Adirondacks, or the "bark eaters" for the manner in which they used tree bark as a food supplement. The band was enslaved for some time but managed to flee the Adirondacks and retrace its journey until its members once again reached Lake Ontario.

The Adirondacks pursued them in their light birchbark canoes and were on the verge of attacking the slower refugees before a great wind rose from the west and overturned the pursuers' boats, drowning them beneath turbulent waters. The refugees reached shore at the mouth of the Oswego River. Along the banks of the river, they built their village, and as time went along, they expanded throughout the region.

Generations later, they became six distinct political entities with well-defined territories but with a common culture and singular language, with regional and national dialects. The Iroquois grew from the southwestern migrants, but the Haudenosaunee (the "People Building the Longhouse") came much later, with the formation of the Confederacy, long after their initial arrival in the northeast. One of the six, the Ska-ru-re ("Shirt-Wearers," or Tuscarora), departed for unexplained reasons for the south, where they settled east of the Appalachians in what is now North Carolina.

The nations took their names from their respective territories or a geographical characteristic of the land. The Mohawks, in the Iroquois language, are the Kaiienkehaka, or "People of the Flint," while their immediate relatives to the west are the Onyota'a-ka, the "People of the Standing Stone," the Oneidas. Those who lived in the center of Iroquois territory are the Ononda-ge, the "People of the Hills," or the Onondaga. To their west, in the great marshlands south of Lake Ontario, are the Gayohkohnyoh, the "Dwellers of the Swamp Lands," or the Cayugas. Farthest west are the Onondawahgah, the "People of the Great Hill," also called the Senecas.

From these groups would arise a distinctive people whose language, culture, spirituality, and technology were defined by the land in which they lived. The archaeological evidence as to when the Iroquois ancestors arrived in the northeast is vague. The division of the Cherokee from the Iroquois, according to linguistic factors, suggests 3500–4000 B.C.E. By at least the year 1000 B.C.E., the Iroquois had a firm hold on millions of acres of land south of the St. Lawrence and north of the Susquehanna. This was a fluid culture by design, grafting new products, ideas, and technologies onto the older stocks.

Corn arrived from the west and forever altered the Iroquois diet and economy, but it may well have been a food source known to them in their trading ventures into the continental interior. The Iroquois were also willing to undertake long journeys to obtain other goods such as whale meat, seashells, and birch bark.

The origin story reveals a continent well populated by human beings for thousands of years prior to the arrival of the Europeans. Certainly, the territory that became the homelands of the Haudenosaunee had been marked with human presence long before the Iroquois colonized the region, but the oral traditions do not speak of a war to cleanse the area of any other people. While the land is said to have been fertile, it is curiously void of other nations, who might have driven the refugees back to the southwest, defeated them in battle, or, like the Adirondacks, placed them in a condition of servitude. It is also interesting that the lower reaches of the St. Lawrence River had a significant human population sufficient to subdue the ancestors of the Iroquois, but there is no description of what should have been, according to climate and fertility, a land south of the river better suited for settlement and natural resource exploitation.

The migration story is, at its conclusion, an epic tale meant to resolve the need for place and belonging. It affirms certain anthropological data as to language roots and hard geographical data about the waters and lands through which the refugees traveled. It connects the Cherokee and the Iroquois linguistically, which affirms at least part of the story, while providing a rough estimate as to when the common ancestors were in the Ohio region. The story also acknowledges the biological and cultural relationship of other Iroquoian peoples who never inhabited the central homelands in New York State but who grew into distinct entities in their own respective areas.

There were also periods in Iroquois history when they expanded or retracted the areas under their control, depending upon variances such as warfare, internal strife, or climatic changes. Towns would have been built far from the main communities in central New York when conditions warranted, but could be abandoned in times of stress. Such was the case with the Mohawks, who had, long before European contact, thriving villages in the St. Lawrence River and Lake Champlain valleys, which, although the people may have left for one reason or another, were remembered and affirmed as evidence the Mohawks had never ceded jurisdiction in those regions.

The migration story ranks with the Skywoman epic and the establishment of the Haudenosaunee Confederacy as critical elements in the Iroquois oral tradition. The Skywoman epic is the most important legend among the Haudenosaunee. It tells not only about the formation of the Earth but the arrival of the human soul from the sky world. The concept of creation and Earth as feminine stem from the Skywoman story. Virtually all contemporary Iroquois artists make use of this epic in their work. These stories are firmly believed by the Iroquois as actual events that took place in time and space and are as truthful in their telling as the Bible or the Koran. In recent times the origin stories have been referred to in order to explain cosmological phenomenon such as solar eclipses, climatic shifts, and the inundation of much of the earth's land by massive floods.

In 1996 the Lakota philosopher Vine Deloria Jr., with the help of the American Indian Science and Engineering Society (AISES), organized an Origins conference in Boulder, Colorado, to bring together traditional scholars from a number of indigenous nations, ranging from the Maya of Guatemala to the Inuit of the north shore of Alaska. AISES made a decided attempt to include as diverse an array of presenters as possible from all regions of the continent. Four years later, the Boulder gathering took place. The sessions were held in the southwest since that region had not only the largest concentration of Native communities, but had a large, primarily urban aboriginal population from virtually every indigenous group in North America.

His concern was the casual dismissal of Native oral traditions by American academia. His own knowledge as to this traditional discipline had led him to question the geophysical, ethnological, and archaeological assumptions of Western science. His own people had, despite generations of active suppression, retained an intimate understanding about the world around them far beyond what could have otherwise been expected given the enforced American-style schooling, physical displacement, and high mortality rates suffered by the keepers of the legends, the elders.

Deloria believed what he had been told by the Lakota knowledge keepers about where they came from and when. He had hosted, in 1992, a conference about stars. The Lakota presenters at that event were able to use the University of Colorado's planetarium to align the stars in the sky in their exact position at the time the ancestors of the Lakotas entered the Great Plains from the west.

The Lakotas said a cluster of stars were in a specific position of the nighttime sky at a certain time of the year, near the sacred mountain called Bear Butte in Wyoming (also referred to as the Devil's Tower). When the planetarium's computer was programmed with all of the relevant data as dictated by the Lakotas and cross-referenced as to latitude-longitude and various astronomical information, they were able to see the night sky the way it looked to those people long ago. The Lakota star knowledge set not only the place, but also the exact year when they entered what would become their homelands.

Other AISES conference delegates discussed animals and plants within the circle of traditional knowledge. One of the anticipated results of the conference was a discussion of the Bering Strait theory, the great myth that had become entrenched in American texts and in classrooms as the most accepted explanation as to how humans first came to the western hemisphere. Despite the absence of hard physical evidence, the Bering Strait theory was set in place and was often cited by opponents of Native nations as proof that everyone in America was a recent immigrant, therefore justifying, in their minds, the termination of indigenous rights as distinct from any other ethnic group.

The small Iroquois delegation, consisting of Cayuga Nation Chief Jake Thomas, Mohawk Nation Chief Jake Swamp, Joanne Shenandoah of the Oneida Nation, and I, were intrigued by the creation stories from other Native nations. Perhaps there were answers to our questions of where the ancestors of the Iroquois originated and how to put the Bering Strait theory to rest.

The conference involved speakers from the Anishnabe (Ojibway), Dine (Navajo), Maya, Lakota, Cheyenne, Inuit, Iroquois, and Pueblo Nations. Its structure was designed to adhere to traditional methods of learning, meaning there would be no mechanical recordings (unless the speaker otherwise agreed), no note taking, no interruptions during the presentations, and no follow-up questions, except those addressed to the speaker outside of the meeting room. Each presenter would talk for as long as he or she deemed appropriate. The intent was to have the audience give its entire attention to the speaker with minimal distractions. Patience would also be called for as the stories took considerable time to relate and were marked by geographical, celestial, floral, and faunal details that sustained the particular narrative. These were the truths as to the origins of the hemisphere's first peoples as experienced by them and then as passed from generation to generation, until they became part of a Native nation's sacred teachings. The speakers agreed to share this information because of Vine Deloria's assurances that in doing so, they would not be challenged or have their stories show up in an academic treatise, insulated from the power inherent in the spoken word. Hence the above conditions.

The session began with a general discussion of the Bering Strait myth. There is no account in any Native creation story that tells of the crossing from Asia to America over a narrow land bridge during the frigid times of the Ice Age. If the current theory as to when people arrived in the Americas is to be believed, it would had to have taken place while much of North America was under glaciers, with thicknesses as great as two miles. The concentration of the planet's waters in the glaciers retained vast quantities of water sufficient to have the oceans recede far beyond their current shores and uncovering land masses now far below the sea's surface. One of these sections was the land bridge between Siberia and Alaska. It was at that time that migrants allegedly crossed over, pursuing large mammals as they unknowingly entered what was, for humans, a new land.

But before they reached Alaska the wandering band, after leaving their central Asian homelands, had to cross a series of mountain ranges in eastern Siberia, which stretched for thousands of miles. This land was trackless, bitterly cold, and hostile in every way to human survival. By superhuman effort, the band may have overcome starvation, death, and despair before reaching the shores of the Bering Sea. They would have had to slowly move through treacherous swamps and stamina-sucking bogs in pursuit of the meager game that dared to make this inhospitable region their home. Once the band reached firm ground, its members faced the Kaiyuh and Kuskokwim mountain ranges before confronting the Alaska and Coast ranges. They would have had to skirt around Denali Mountain (Mt. McKinley, 20,320 feet high) and the formidable Granite Range, with eight peaks over 10,000 feet in height, capped by massive Mt. Logan at 19,850 feet. Then they would have seen a sight to inspire awe and fear in the most intrepid of hunters: a great wall of ice so high that only the tallest of mountaintops broke through its surface.

The theory goes on with this ridiculous tale by proposing the idea that a narrow corridor somehow existed between two sections of the glacier sufficiently wide enough to allow humans and animals to walk thousands of miles from Alaska to the Great Plains in the American West. Nothing is said by the theory's proponents about the hurricane winds that would have crossed the channel or the flesh-killing cold caused by having to trudge through the ice. All of this was nonsensical to the 1996 Origins conference delegates. Omitted was the linguistic diversity of aboriginal Americans, which would have required many more thousands of years to develop. Also left out was the glaring abscence of any hard, irrefutable physical evidence to support the Bering Strait theory.

It was up to the conference speakers to put the pieces of the origin puzzle together, relying on exclusively Native sources which, we were convinced, would be supported by those archaeologists willing to challenge the Asian migration story and begin their search using our stories as to where to look.

We heard first from the Inuit. Their stories tell of a time when they lived in a more temperate climate in a land of trees and plants. In this land they hunted large mammals, some of which had great protruding tusks and elongated snouts. Their story reveals a most intriguing detail that explains why huge creatures such as the mammoth were later found entombed in ice with vegetation in their mouths, as if they had been flash frozen in the middle of eating. The Inuit say the earth shifted, literally within minutes, and that before a day had passed their territory had changed from trees and open seas to permafrost, ice, and snow. The only way some of them survived was to adhere to the warnings of their spiritual leaders, who had dreamed of the earth's radical movement and had persuaded many of them to retreat deep into the caves in the mountains of northern Alaska. There they dwelled for generations, making occasional ventures onto the surface of the earth to hunt and forage. On some of their hunts they found creatures frozen rigid when the temperatures dropped far beyond any animal's ability to endure.

The shifting of the earth was affirmed by the Cheyenne. Their origin story also tells of a time when they lived in the Rocky Mountains in present-day Wyoming before making their way to the northeast, where they encountered Europeans in the early seventeenth century. When they departed the woodlands because of disease and warfare, they retraced the steps of their ancestors and returned to the Great Plains and the foothills of the Rockies, relying on the most ancient of stories. They also tell of a sudden climatic change taking place within a day's span and that the only way they survived was to enter the great caves in the Laramie Mountains in the southeastern part of the state. Go deep enough into the earth, and one will find natural warmth sufficient to preserve life, even as the world remains frozen above. The Cheyennes said the caves were of sufficient size to keep small herds of buffalo, with food for the animals coming from harvesting ventures to the surface during the short weeks when the grasslands were free of snow and frost. Once the climate warmed, the ancestors of the Cheyenne emerged from their terra sanctuaries to resume their Plains culture lifestyles.

Among the Iroquois, there are also stories of caves, places which provided a haven from the elements and security in times of war. The northeastern dwellers tell of living deep in the earth before emerging into this world in the western part of New York State at a certain place on the eastern edges of Canandaigua Lake. The stories tell of an underground passage that connects different parts of Iroquois territory from Mohawk land west of the Hudson River to the Senecas 200 miles westward.

Similar stories about following a tubular passage from the earth's depths to the surface are retained by many other Native nations such as the Hopi, the Dine (Navajo), and the Lakota. They also put to rest the idea that humans were not here prior to the last Ice Age, while providing archaeologists with a new direction in which to apply their research skills.

The Pueblos provided an answer to the origin of the Iroquois. One of their stories tells of a large number of their people who had left the Rio Grande area many hundreds of years ago, departing for the northeast. There is no explanation given as to why the group left other than a desire to find new territory, perhaps in response to overpopulation in the river valleys of the southwest. If that is so, the Iroquois delegation wondered, where did the Pueblos come from?

The response was consistent with the origin story of the Dine (Navajo). That nation is described by anthropologists as an Athabaskan people with close linguistic and biological relatives south of the Arctic Circle in the Alberta–Northwest Territory region of Canada. Did this not sustain the argument that the Dine were northern peoples who followed the Asian migration route from the northwest to the southwest? Not so, explained the Dine. They told of coming from the far south, beyond the Rio Grande, in a land of forests and great flowering plants. From there they settled in the drier lands before moving north during a time of warmth for the entire continent. Only when it grew colder in their adopted homes did they retreat to return to the southwest.

This was affirmed by the Pueblos, who also told of coming from the south in a territory marked by hills, great forests, and large plants. The Pueblo presenter was very specific as to the kind of flowers and other plants in that faraway land. The flow of human activity in North America seems to emanate from the strip of land that connects the two Americas, an observation which the Mayan speaker endorsed.

The origin story of the Mayas, long held to be the "grandfathers" of all native peoples in the Americas, explained where the trail began. The presenter said the ancestors of the Mayas came from a fertile land located to the west of what is now Nicaragua. That land was the place from which all Native peoples came. A massive earthquake caused a great flood to sweep over the land, which then sank beneath the Pacific Ocean, causing the deaths of most of its inhabitants. Those who survived used watercrafts to sail and paddle to the east, where, after many days at sea, they reached the coast of Central America and from there journeyed to the north and south.

Such, then, was the logical answer as to the entry of humans into America. The flooding of a land mass as described by the Maya also affirmed another universal legend among Native peoples, stories which tell of a time when much of the earth was under water and beneath a heavy layer of clouds which prevented those with eyes from seeing the sun or the nighttime sky. Only when the moon was torn from the earth and thrust into the sky did the clouds disperse, enabling the beings of the world to see the stars above.

Chapter 2

Akwesasne

History among the Mohawks is a highly personal matter since it involves the life stories of a people with deep spiritual connections to the place in which they have grown. When a Mohawk person speaks of his or her community, it becomes a narrative in which they carry the experiences of their ancestors across the generations.

Akwesasne is a community rich in story: tragic, comedic, and dramatic. By intertwining the oral and written records, a compelling epic emerges, one that is about more than mere survival—it is about perseverance through decades of adversity.

Like all Native peoples, whatever is begins and ends with the land in which the story takes root. Since the Akwesasne region is particularly fertile in the way of natural resources, it follows that its history would be equally prolific.

The Mohawks were not the first people to call the area their home. Those who came before the Mohawks were of the Algonkian family: hunters, fisher-men, and trappers. They were attracted to the region primarily because of its biological diversity and physical beauty.

Located at the confluence of the Grasse, Racquette, St. Regis, Salmon, and St. Lawrence Rivers, it carries a tremendous water flow from the Adirondack Mountains, which is filtered by the largest freshwater marshes in the north-east. Birds of all kinds, from sharp-eyed eagles to the broad-winged great blue heron, had found excellent fishing in the crystal waters along the edges of the marsh, which also contained the lodges of hundreds of muskrats and beavers.

There are over thirty islands at Akwesasne, ranging in size from the half-acre Hen Island to the flat tilling fields of St. Regis and Yellow Islands. The St. Lawrence is squeezed through narrow channels on either side of five-mile-long Cornwall Island. The remnants of the powerful Long Sault rapids remain in the northern channel, while the southern section gently flows against the clay shores of the U.S. mainland.

In former times the islands were a resting ground for herds of caribou and deer as they swam across the river during the autumn migrations. There also were rumbling bears, bellowing elks, howling wolves, and yowling cougars, all of which disappeared when the area was colonized in the early nineteenth century.

An abundance of physical evidence clearly shows that the Akwesasne region has long been Iroquois territory. From pottery shards to burial mounds, there is every indication that a series of thriving communities flourished along the river. The elaborate rituals that defined Mohawk life could only have been sustained by a people who had the time and food resources to participate in ceremonies that lasted as long as a week. The complex social life of the Mohawks was quite different from that of their Algonkian neighbors since the Iroquois were an agriculturally based culture, with corn as the primary staple.

According to oral tradition, there was a large Mohawk village on the peninsula that juts into the place where the St. Lawrence and St. Regis Rivers meet. It would have been logical to expect the Mohawks to have made use of the location by having a palisaded village there as it would have enabled them to monitor river traffic and exercise control over the movement of goods and people upon the St. Lawrence. Across the St. Regis River, to the south of the village, the Mohawks buried their dead in earthen mounds since it was believed that restless spirits found it impossible to cross wide bodies of water.

A Catholic church now stands on the point in St. Regis Village. From its high steeple there is a sweeping view of the St. Lawrence River, which is the main water route into the continental interior. The decision by the parish to place its facility at the point was typical of the Catholic Church, which grafted its buildings on sites which had historical or religious significance for the Native community to which the church was administering.

By the end of the sixteenth century, the Mohawks had retreated from Akwesasne. Various European-born plagues and the onset of war with the Algonkians and their allies had wiped out the population, compelling the people to retreat to the Mohawk Valley area in central New York State to recover.

Generations would pass before the Mohawks returned to the region. They did so first by constructing a Catholic community called Kahnawake across the river from Montreal in 1669. Seventy years later, the soils and animal resources had been depleted enough for some Mohawks to consider leaving for new lands. They had been through Akwesasne many times on hunting and trade expeditions and recalled it as a place where Mohawks had lived before.

By 1747, enough Mohawks had moved to Akwesasne for it to be called a community. Eight years later, in 1754, the church sent its first priest, Father Pierre Billiard, to tend to the spiritual needs of the Mohawks. There were a sufficient number of families to formally establish a parish in 1755.

Although the Mohawks had their own names for the rivers and islands at Akwesasne, the church elected to name the community after St. Francis Regis, a Jesuit priest from Toulouse, France (1597–1640), who administered to the poor of that city. He also founded a home for prostitutes called the "Daughters of Refuge." His determination to enter areas suffering from plagues was a source of contention with the other Jesuits, who felt his acts were reckless and cast a bad light on the rest of them. It was his wish to travel to Quebec to aid in the conversion of the Iroquois, but he died before he could realize his life's dream.

The Mohawk name for the area, Akwesasne, refers to the drumming sound made by partridges, which roosted on the branches of the pine trees once abundant along the river shores. Quick work was made of those trees, which were highly prized by the British and French navies to be used for building their ships. The 200-foot-tall white pines were among the first species to be wiped out because of the market demands of the Europeans. Since the partridges no longer roosted in great numbers, calling the community St. Regis instead of Akwesasne made sense to some, with the inclusive Mohawk name not coming into wide usage again until the 1970s.

For most of their recorded history the Mohawks were referred to as St. Regis Indians. As students in one of the last Native boarding schools in Canada in the late 1960s, our small Akwesasne contingent were called the "St. Regis boys." Our reservation lacrosse teams also were labeled as having come from St. Regis, although we knew nothing about the person under whose name we lived. The church was not fond of teaching its history beyond the North American martyrs and the trials of Kateri Tekakwitha, the saintly Mohawk girl who was said to have given her life for the church and whom we were expected to emulate. It would have been difficult to wrangle guilt from the life of St. Regis as our ancestors did not have a chance to make him a martyr, but his failure to come to our territory was just as well since he would have brought the plague virus with him and inadvertently killed off the people he wanted to convert.

From the founding of the mission to fairly recently the history of the Mohawks of Akwesasne was intertwined with the church. It was Mohawks who built a wooden church, then a second one when the first burned down, and yet a third, this time of stone, when number two was also consumed by fire. It is very likely my ancestors learned the skill of stonecutting and the art of masonry in 1793 when the third church was constructed. It stands today, overlooking the waterway approaches to the community to the east, a testament to the determination of the Mohawks to set things right as well as an affirmation of their Christian faith. Over 200 years later my family, most of whom are masons, continue to work on the church, insuring that the labor of generations past endures.

Given Akwesasne's strategic location, it was bound to attract attention from military commanders and politicians vying for control over the most important water route in eastern North America. The Mohawks who resettled in Akwesasne were certainly aware of this and sought to use the location to their advantage. They were not prepared to retreat to the mountains since being actively involved in the political dynamics of the time was a source of real power for all Iroquois.

While the Mohawks were settling in to enjoy their freshwater fish, the French and English were at each other's throats in yet another conflict called the French and Indian War as well as the Seven Years' War. The Mohawks were called upon by both sides to fulfill their obligations as allies and lead the European armies into battle. While the men of Akwesasne might have been more concerned during that particular year with building projects and hunting, their kin at Kahnawake got involved.

The Mohawks from that community were persuaded by the French to serve as scouts during the Lake George campaign, which took place in 1755. They knew there was an excellent chance they would encounter other Mohawks fighting for the English but believed they could refrain from actually killing their southern relatives. Plans made prior to a battle are often discarded or ignored during the actual fighting, and so it was at Lake George. Mohawk fought Mohawk, Mohawks killed their blood kin, and when the battle was over, the Kahnawake contingent learned someone among them had taken the life of the great Theyanoguin (Hendrick), one of the foremost Native leaders of the 1700s and the man who, just the year before, had the British colonies emulate the Haudenosaunee by uniting into one great confederacy.

Akwesasne had no part in Theyanoguin's death, but the animosity of their Mohawk Valley relatives toward the Kahnawakes would continue for many years. In 1776–1777, when the valley dwellers were compelled to leave their homes at the edge of bayonet-wielding militias, they found refuge at Akwesasne, ignoring Kahnawake altogether.

When the British commanders dismissed the advice of their Native allies, they stumbled into ambushes, just as Braddock had done in western Pennsylvania in June 1755. If Braddock had taken the advice of the commander of the Virginia militia, a young man named George Washington, over 1,000 of his soldiers would not have walked into the trap set by the French and their Native allies, many of whom were Iroquois.

With the assistance of Mohawk fighters the British scored victories at Ft. Niagara and Lake George. It is also said a singular Mohawk scout led the British troops up an obscure riverside trail to the Plains of Abraham near Quebec City in 1759, where the fate of North America was determined in a single battle. At its conclusion, General James Wolfe, the victorious British commander, was dead after having been shot in the chest, while his French counterpart, Louis Montcalm, was slowly dying from a similar wound.

Once the French surrendered their Quebec colony to England, the Mohawks were placed in an awkward position. Prior to the loss of New France, they were important middlemen, courted by both powers since they held sway over many Native nations, but no longer. They were now in a struggle to protect their homelands against the colonists, whose appetite for Iroquois territory was without limit.

At the urging of the Iroquois, and as a direct result of Pontiac's War in the Great Lakes region, the British enacted the Royal Proclamation of 1763, which outlawed the sale of Native lands to anyone, except the central government in London. This was followed by the 1768 Treaty of Ft. Stanwix, which set a firm border between the Natives and the settlers, fixed along the ridges of the Appalachian Mountains on a north-south axis and ending at the Mohawk River. Lands to the north were left to further negotiations between the Haudenosaunee and Britain, but most of the uncharted territory was identified on the maps from that era as Mohawk. There were simply too many conflicting land grants to set a permanent boundary line.

Akwesasne was dragged into the land controversies along with every other Iroquois community. To protect its interests the governing council on the territory became a part of the Seven Nations group, a loose alliance of Native Christian communities located along the St. Lawrence River. Some were composed of a mixture of Indian people such as the Algonkians, Nippissings, and Mohawks of Two Mountains (Oka-Kanehsatake). These three joined the Hurons of Lorette, the Abenakis of St. Francis, the Mohawks of Kahnawake, and the Onondagas-Oneidas of Oswegatchie. Since it was a relatively new member, with many of its inhabitants coming directly from Kahnawake, Akwesasne was deemed an extension of the older group.

During the American Revolution the Mohawks attempted to secure neutrality in the fight between brothers, but the British expected them to abide by their covenant chain commitment, in which they pledged fidelity to the Crown. The covenant chain was indicative of a formal Haudenosaunee-British treaty relationship dating from 1677. The symbolic chain is made of silver to prevent decay and is to be renewed or "polished" when the Haudenosaunee meet with representatives from Britain or its successor states, Canada and the United States. The chain not only binds the nations together but represents an acknowledgment of the political sovereignty of the Haudenosaunee. The rebels respected the power of the Confederacy and either wanted the Iroquois to stay out of the war or to ally themselves with the colonies. Treaties of peace and friendship were entered into between the colonies and the Confederacy at Ft. Pitt and Albany in 1775, the first formal international agreements secured by the rebels, but there was no way to conduct military campaigns without entering Iroquois territory and thereby bringing them into the war.

The Oneidas were the first to break ranks when the warrior group, under the influence of Reverend Samuel Kirkland, declared for the rebels. The Mohawks who remained in the Mohawk Valley were under the leadership of Little Abraham, but try as they might, they could not find a way to sustain their neutral stance. Joseph Brant, a Mohawk from the Bear Clan village of Canajoharie and a protégé of Sir William Johnson, used his strong ties with the English military to secure a captain's commission in the army. He spent weeks in London during the winter of 1775–1776, lobbying for the Crown to commit to aggressive support for the Iroquois should they elect to fight. He returned to America in time to take part in the Battle of Long Island before returning to Iroquois territory, where he visited dozens of communities in an attempt to win them over to Britain.

By that time, most Mohawks had long left the valley area because they were being pressured by settlers and land speculators to sell their remaining holdings and move west. Small groups of Mohawks left for Akwesasne or the Ohio region but were bitter about the loss of their homelands. Brant said that once the British had defeated the rebels, the terms of the 1768 Ft. Stanwix Treaty would be carried out, which would have protected the Iroquois from losing more land. The Americans made similar assurances, but given that the primary cause of the war was the struggle over land, it was unlikely they would be able to abide by their promises.

Brant did not travel to Akwesasne since the Mohawks there had no doubt about which side they would support. The American rebels were a distant people, while the Mohawks were in constant contact with the British. From their homes alongside the St. Lawrence they could watch flotillas of British troops work their way up the river to strengthen the garrisons at Forts Niagara and Oswego. The hundreds of redcoats, with their fifes, bagpipes, cannons, and drums, were an impressive display of power by one of the strongest armies in the world.

At Kahnawake the Americans had an agent who was trying to counter Brant. He was Louis Cook, an African-Abenaki man raised by the Mohawks at Kahnawake but committed to the rebel cause. He traveled among the Oneidas and Mohawks gathering information, sowing dissension, and looking for men to enlist as scouts for the American army.

Cook was also known as Atiatonharonkwen, which meant, appropriately, "he pulls down the people," and that he did. His espionage work for the rebels began in 1775, even as the Confederacy was negotiating peace agreements with the colonies. Cook was welcomed in New England for his anti-British actions because of the highly detailed nature of his reports to the American commanders. He caused sufficient divisions at Kahnawake to win some of the men to his side, but it was his recruitment of large numbers of Oneidas which resulted in Congress giving him a colonel's commission in the U.S. Army, the first black man to serve as an officer in the American military. Perhaps General Washington did not know Cook was a part of the French-Native ambush team that almost cost him his life when they destroyed General Braddock's army near Fort Pitt in 1755. Washington was a leader of the colonial troops and, while targeted by Native snipers, managed to escape the slaughter with only his coat pierced by bullets.

Colonel Cook was not successful in winning Akwesasne to his side. The Mohawks there chose to support the British, beginning by giving food and supplies to loyalists fleeing to Canada in fear of their lives. Many of the Scots-English there elected to remain next to Akwesasne, where they built communities named after the towns and districts in the British Isles. The only major battle in which the Mohawks of Akwesasne took a notable part was the fiasco at Saratoga, where they witnessed one of the most inept military campaigns of all time. Chastised by General Burgoyne's officers for not being as brutal as the Native fighters from the Great Lakes, the Akwesasne contingent picked up their muskets and went home to harvest their crops, leaving the British to the mercy of the Americans and their Oneida allies.

While the Mohawks of Akwesasne did not take a prominent role in the war, they did accommodate their displaced relatives from the Mohawk Valley. Captain Brant had proved to be a formidable commander in the field, with his fighters waging an extremely effective guerilla war in New York and Pennsylvania. Hundreds of farms were torched and dozens of communities destroyed, while thousands of patriots were forced to flee their homes as refugees. Brant was driving the Americans to their knees by denying them badly needed food from some of the most productive areas in the northeast.

In response to Brant's intrusions, Washington ordered the year's most important military action in 1779 when he sent General John Sullivan and over 5,000 troops to invade Confederate territory and break the back of the Iroquois. Sullivan's harvest season campaign was effective in burning most of the Seneca and Cayuga towns, while laying waste to thousands of acres of corn and fruit crops. He drove thousands of Iroquois from their homes to starve through the terrible winter of 1779–1780. Far from defeating the Iroquois, his actions caused them to strike back with a vengeance. What remained of the frontier in 1779 was set afire in 1780, and the Iroquois were prepared to fight even longer. What they could not know was that the British had lost the will to continue the struggle and had agreed to cease military operations pending a peace treaty, which was signed in Paris in 1783.

The Iroquois were enraged by this act of duplicity, which left them at the mercy of the Americans. Large sections of Haudenosaunee territory, including parts belonging to the loyal Oneidas, were given to U.S. officers and soldiers in lieu of pay. New York divided Mohawk territory into quadrants, which were then sold to speculators who were not above paying kickbacks to accommodating politicians.

One of the largest sections sold off was to Alexander Macomb, a New York City–based trader. Over six million acres of Oneida-Mohawk land were purchased from New York, which had incurred heavy debts as a result of the war.

One day, the Mohawks of Akwesasne woke to find a surveying crew measuring its way across the area. When asked what they were doing, the surveyors replied that the land had been sold and that they were simply doing their jobs by defining the limits of the new owner's territory. When the Mohawks protested at Albany that the land was being sold without their permission, a minor concession was made to set aside "six miles square" around the village of St. Regis, and nothing more.

Colonel Cook was then living at Akwesasne, having good cause not to return to Kahnawake. Joining him was a former American soldier named William Gray. They were asked to serve as interpreters for the Mohawks with the State over the land issue. Instead, Gray and Cook accepted bribes from Albany officials and set their names, along with Thomas Williams, a Mohawk from Kahnawake who had moved to Akwesasne, and Ohnaweio ("Good Stream"), a name which is not one of chief's titles among the Mohawk, to the 1796 Seven Nations of Canada Treaty, which confined the Mohawks to a small reservation along the St. Lawrence River and an annual annuity of a few hundred dollars.

Neither Cook nor Gray had any authority to cede anything except their personal property. They were not delegated by the Mohawks to sell land, nor were they representatives of the Seven Nations, yet the treaty, for all of its controversy, was signed into law by Washington. The territorial limits of Akwesasne were set, and reservation life had begun. Once the Mohawks had hunted, fished, and camped over millions of acres of pristine forests and fertile river valleys, as free to move about as any people had ever been. After 1796 they were bound to the marshes, islands, and rock-strewn fields of a small reservation, where they were numbed by an alien faith and subdued by government officials who treated them as domestic dependents removed, barely, from a state of savagery by the grace of a grim and jealous God.

The Akwesasne Mohawks were governed by a system of "life chiefs," modeled after the traditional council, which consisted of nine male chiefs and nine clanmothers, each one of whom was assigned a faithkeeper, or spiritual advisor. The life chiefs were also called the "longhairs" for their distinctive appearance. There were three chiefs from each of the Mohawk clans: Bear, Wolf, and Turtle. They were nominated for office by the clanmothers, a selection which had to be endorsed by their respective clans before being passed on to the community council to be either endorsed or rejected.

The leaders served for life but were subject to removal for breach of communal standards or physical illness. While they adhered to the ancient governance methods, they did not possess the formal titles that are an integral part of the Mohawk Nation Council. Nor were the life chiefs representative of the Mohawk people other than those who resided at Akwesasne. The council did have the authority to adjudicate disputes, conduct relations with external agencies, disperse justice, and allocate resources. Unlike the Mohawk Nation Council, the life chiefs did not perform traditional ceremonies since they were Catholic. The original nine chiefs were expanded to twelve in 1806 when the Onondagas-Oneidas of Oswegatchie (near present-day Ogdensburg, New York) were forcibly dispersed by New York State, then given refuge in the eastern district of Akwesasne. They brought with them their own community council, which followed the clan system. In recognition of this the Mohawks added three clan representatives, Deer, Beaver, and Snipe, to the original nine.

Millions of acres of Mohawk land had already been carved up and sold to speculators long before the 1796 Seven Nations of Canada Treaty, and New York State was not willing to delay the extinguishment of Mohawk land rights by entering into negotiations with the life chiefs. New York found it far easier to negotiate land cession agreements with a smaller group. Shortly after the Seven Nations of Canada Treaty, it once again sought territorial concessions with Williams, Cook, and Gray. Those three were designated as trustees for the St. Regis Indians (a system which was codified into the St. Regis Tribal Council by an act of the New York State legislature in 1892).

In the first decades of the nineteenth century the trustees were given limited administrative powers by New York, which included the distribution of the annual annuities owed the community as a result of the land sales. The original reservation boundary was, by treaty, to consist of six miles square around the village of St. Regis, a mile square section around the mineral springs on the Grasse River in the town of Massena, and hayfields on either side of the Grasse from the springs to the St. Lawrence River. Since the land surveys were imprecise, the reservation boundaries extended north of the 45th degree of longitude into the British colony of Upper Canada and conflicted with land grants made by the Crown to the Mohawks. Those Mohawks residing under British jurisdiction held possession of dozens of islands in the St. Lawrence from Ogdensburg to Lake St. Francis, a 22,000-acre tract in the Quebec township of Dundee and a mile-wide, 18-mile-long section of land from the Ontario riverside hamlet of Glen Walter northward to the village of Martinsburg called the "Nutfield Tract."

The three trustees were given the authority to cede territory from the initial boundaries of Akwesasne through a series of state treaties from 1816 to 1845. Over 10,000 acres of the original 24,000-acre reservation would be lost, including the critical fishing waters of the Grasse River and the lucrative wood mills in the town of Hogansburg.

New York was obligated to pay an annual annuity to the Akwesasne Mohawks and their Kahnawake relatives since that reserve was the seat of the Seven Nations of Canada. Over the objections of Kahnawake its payments were terminated in 1841; henceforth only the "American"-based Mohawks would receive money.

The land cessions entered into by the three trustees took place during a time when the residents of Akwesasne were hard pressed to secure sufficient food to survive. The weakened state of the Mohawks was evident when a series of communal epidemics, such as cholera, typhoid, and smallpox, reduced the population by half from 1820 to 1850. Any income was critical to the purchase of badly needed food supplies.

Beginning in 1813 and continuing for the next few years, a series of bad harvests brought the community close to starvation. The Tambora volcanic explosion of 1815 in Indonesia sent massive amounts of dust into the atmosphere, which in turn cooled the earth and caused heavy frosts in the continental northeast well into June. The short growing season meant essential food crops did not reach full maturity, leaving the Mohawks to rely on lean pickings and making it easy for New York officials to alienate more land.

Added to the food crisis was the War of 1812, which deeply affected Akwesasne. Once again, the men were asked to choose sides: enlist as fighters for the United States, or sustain their alliance with the British. On the whole, Akwesasne elected to fight for the Crown, although individuals such as Louis Cook, William Gray, and Eleazer Williams, the son of Thomas Williams, served as spies and recruiters for the Americans.

The first military victory for the United States occurred at Akwesasne, where the British had a small garrison near the banks of the St. Lawrence River, from which they were able to monitor water traffic. Once hostilities commenced, the Americans organized a militia in the nearby town of French Mills (later named Ft. Covington in recognition of a U.S. general). Relying on the information given to them by William Gray, the Americans caught the British by surprise. After a short battle the garrison surrendered and was marched off as prisoners of war.

The Mohawks felt compelled to support the British, although the image of Iroquois on the loose caused considerable concern among the Americans. This did not prevent the Mohawks from purchasing badly needed food supplies in northern New York State and using Akwesasne's water routes to smuggle their goods into Upper Canada for sale to the British army.

The Mohawks as a whole played a vital role in several battles that determined the fate of British Canada. At the battles of Queenston Heights, Beaver Dam, and Chateauguay the Mohawk contingent was in the midst of the fighting as it turned back the American invaders.

There was, however, considerable ambiguity among the Iroquois regarding their participation in the war. Many believed the British did not merit the alliance of the Six Nations given its abandonment of the Iroquois at the signing of the Treaty of Paris in 1783, which brought the American Revolution to an end but omitted any provision protecting the Native nations. The peace advocates among the Iroquois were opposed to becoming entangled in the British-American hostilities, while the advocates for war saw a chance to regain lost status and perhaps secure protection for their rapidly diminishing land holdings.

Akwesasne was most vulnerable to the passions of the moment. The Americans were making effective use of the international border which divided the community into factions. Those residing on the U.S. side provided intelligence to the American authorities, while the Mohawks north of the border took up arms and fought with distinction at Beaver Dam, where a combined Iroquois force defeated an American army, capturing over 500 U.S. troops.

At Chateauguay a small group of Akwesasne fighters from the U.S. side fought against their Mohawk cousins from Kahnawake, while another Akwesasne group operated a scouting service for the British at Crysler's Farm, where the Tyendinaga Mohawks took part in their only conflict of the entire war.

On August 17, 1813, at Ball's Farm on the Niagara peninsula, the Iroquois of the Grand River and their British allies repelled a combined U.S.–Iroquois army attack, forcing the invaders to retreat to nearby Ft. George. It was the first time since the Revolution that Iroquois had fought their kin. Although the outcome of the battle was not a decisive engagement, it did solidify the differences between the "Canadian" and "American" Iroquois and would have significant ramifications for generations.

One tangible result of the War of 1812 at Akwesasne was the permanent imposition of the international border through its lands. With that came the division of the community along that line. For the next century the Mohawks north of the line would be governed by an indigenous council of 12 life chiefs, while those to the south had as their leaders a council composed of three trustees elected by popular ballot for a rotating term of three years. Initially restricted to males over 21 years of age, voter eligibility was gradually expanded to include women, then was lowered to tribal members 18 years and older with American residency. No Canadian-based Mohawks were allowed to vote.

All land cession agreements made between New York State and the Akwesasne Mohawks were secured using the trustee method. Whenever the Mohawks were in desperate conditions, they ceded the only commodity they had: land. During and after the War of 1812 the community barely endured a series of crop failures followed by outbreaks of typhoid, cholera, and smallpox, which killed hundreds of Mohawks. By 1850, the population was half of what it had been in 1812.

Saving Canada was not enough. The British authorities also hacked away at Akwesasne's land base. Over 20,000 acres were lost when the Dundee tract in the Quebec district was taken in 1882. The Americans had whittled down the U.S. side to 14,000 acres by 1845, seven years after they had tried to remove all Iroquois to Kansas under the terms of the first Treaty of Buffalo Creek, an agreement so blatantly fraudulent it had to be renegotiated four years later.

A group of Akwesasne Mohawks traveled to the west to examine the Kansas lands, where most of them died. Those who returned effectively persuaded their kin to remain in northern New York. The state, however, was determined to effect a permanent division among the Mohawks.

The lives of the Mohawks were deeply affected by the overall changes taking place in North American society. Up until the War of 1812, the Akwesasne Mohawks secured employment as expert canoeists and fur traders with the North West Fur Company as well as with the Hudson's Bay Company. Mohawks had reached the far west, intermarrying with Natives in the Idaho region and then establishing their own settlement, along with their Kahnawake relatives, in western Alberta.

When the Mohawk participation in the fur trade diminished after the merger of the North West Fur and Hudson's Bay companies in 1821, they turned to logging, fishing, basketry, and farming as means of making a living. During the winter months, many Mohawk families left the reservation to work as lumberjacks in the forests of the Adirondacks or eastern Ontario. During early spring they used gill nets to catch fish during the annual runs, while in the summer they worked their small farms or served as river guides through the St. Lawrence rapids.

Epidemics remained a serious problem throughout the nineteenth century. The plagues took many lives and prevented the population from expanding beyond a couple of thousand residents. Many of the current mannerisms that characterize an Akwesasne Mohawk (such as a reluctance to shake hands, embrace others, or turning aside while speaking) can be attributed to the communal diseases of the 1800s.

Mohawks enlisted in the Union Army during the American Civil War, although they were initially discouraged from doing so. The small bands of Mohawks were indistinguishable from their blue-clad comrades, having abandoned the ancient fighting methods and warfare clothing and styles which had caused such great terror among their former adversaries. The Mohawk fighter in the 98th New York State Voluntary Infantry obeyed orders, marched in step, and drilled in units the same as everyone else. Since few Mohawks actually enlisted, there were even fewer casualties, thereby minimizing the effects the war had on the community.

It is interesting to note that one Iroquois, the Seneca engineer Ely Parker, played a key role in the war as aide to General Ulysses S. Grant and penned the terms of surrender signed at Appamattox by generals Grant and Lee. Parker would later become the first Native person to direct the Bureau of Indian Affairs in Washington, D.C.

Important was the need for the Mohawks to reassume their historical position as the "keepers of the eastern door" for the symbolic longhouse of the Six Nations Confederacy. Ever since the Mohawks had been compelled to leave their homes in the Mohawk Valley of central New York during the American Revolution, the Confederacy's Grand Council had to function without the Mohawks having a national capital. The traditional practices, both spiritual and political, took place within an unadorned rectangular building of varying dimensions (dependent on the specific Iroquois community). These so-called longhouses were a remnant of the style used as residences by the Iroquois. Each longhouse (some of which were over 300 feet in length) were divided into separate apartments, one to a family. During the later half of the eighteenth century, the longhouse was replaced by log and planed board homes, but the ancient building style has been retained as a communal gathering place.

The council fire, or central government, of each member of the Six Nations is signified by the use of a span of wampum, or fire. Without this an Iroquois council is without official status. Mohawks from Akwesasne did retain the clan system of government identical in method and design with the traditional customs and procedures, but with a few omissions.

The life chief system at Akwesasne was modeled after the nine-chief, three-clan practices of the national government in the Mohawk Valley. Another difference was the lack of a longhouse at Akwesasne. Those few Mohawks who elected to take part in the indigenous rituals did so by traveling to Onondaga, the Grand River, or to one of the distant Seneca communities. The Catholic priest kept a close eye on his flock and was quick to condemn any parishioner who was tempted to take part in the "pagan" rituals.

Despite this, in 1888 the Grand Council of the Six Nations designated Akwesasne as the council fire for all the Mohawks. All subsequent chiefs would carry a title name and represent their clan at local and national assemblies of the Six Nations Confederacy.

Fearful that the Mohawks might actually begin to govern Akwesasne as a singular territory, New York State officials acted to make the three trustees into a governing entity called the St. Regis Tribal Council. Through an act of the state's legislature in 1892 the Tribal Council was given limited authority, but sufficient to counter the move toward nationalizing the reservation.

The Canadian government followed suit by creating a "band council" to replace the life chiefs. When the Mohawks on the Canadian side opposed that effort, a contingent of Royal Canadian Mounted Police was sent in to compel the Mohawks to accept federal authority as to the nature of Indian government.

On May 1, 1899, the Mounties arrived at the Akwesasne village of St. Regis. The Mohawks resisted handing over their chiefs to the Mounties, rightfully fearing they would be imprisoned. A Mohawk man, Jake Fire, was shot and killed by the Mounties while they arrested the chiefs, many of whom would spend a year in jail for refusing to surrender their positions.

Elections to the band council were called for, only to have the community vote in the life chiefs. The Canadians persisted, and by the First World War, the band council was firmly in place.

The record of Akwesasne Mohawk service in World War I was limited, unlike that of their relatives at the Six Nations (Oshweken–Grand River) reserve, where a number of Iroquois were awarded citations and medals acknowledging their courage under fire. The veterans returned home to lead the charge against the traditional council that governed Oshweken, working with Canadian officials in 1924 to create a band council system similar to the one in Akwesasne.

As in Akwesasne, the federal government in Ottawa used the Mounties to insure the band council was set in place over the objections of the community. The invasion of Oshweken was also designed to counter the first wave of Native nationalism which had found fertile ground among the Iroquois after the war.

There was a direct connection between the rise of nationalism and the hundreds of Mohawks who had been sent to Indian boarding schools in the United States and Canada. Once there, they were made aware of the conditions in other Native communities with concerns and issues similar to Akwesasne's. At the Carlisle Indian Industrial School, the Thomas Indian School at Spanish, and inside the Mohawk Institute the students learned a fundamental lesson about surviving the harsh conditions of these distant schools: by banding together, they could endure.

From Carlisle alumni came the first national Native organization, the Society of American Indians. Created by Dr. Carlos Montezuma in 1911, a former physician at Carlisle, the Society published a newsletter called "Wassaja," in which calls were made for the abolition of the Bureau of Indian Affairs and the right for Native nations to control their own resources.

A similar group, the Council of Tribes, was formed in 1914 by a Native rights advocate called Ogema Niagara, or Thunderwater. Coming from Ohio, Thunderwater was of uncertain heritage, but his appeals for self-determination echoed those of Montezuma. Thunderwater had considerable support among the Iroquois, particularly at Akwesasne. He sought to restore the traditional council to authority but also emphasized resource management and temperance. The response by the Canadian government was to initiate a campaign to discredit Thunderwater.

He was also opposed by bootleggers and smugglers, then reaping profits by using Akwesasne's open border to bring alcohol into the United States after Prohibition. Smuggling was a way of life along the St. Lawrence long before, and long after, Prohibition. The Mohawks were astute operators aware of market conditions and the rules of supply and demand. If the Americans had a fondness for French lace or wine from Bordeaux, then Akwesasne entrepreneurs found a way to respond to that need; so, too, if the Quebecois desired Virginia tobacco, they could arrange for shipment, minus import duties, through Akwesasne for a reasonable fee.

There had always been a move to unify Akwesasne under a singular indigenous council. Border issues were of growing concern, not only because of the smuggling, but because of the efforts by the United States to restrict entry to Canadian-based Mohawks, many of whom were employed south of the border.

There was cause for celebration when the U.S. courts upheld the rights of Native people to cross the international border for work purposes. In the case *United States ex Rel. Diabo v. McCandless* (Diabo was an ironworker from Kahnawake, but the outcome of his case would impact every Iroquois community) the U.S. Supreme Court ruled, in 1927, that Article 3 of the 1794 Jay Treaty exempted Native people from U.S. immigration laws, a major victory, particularly for the Mohawks of Akwesasne, the residents of whom lived in a state of apprehension whenever they crossed the border, which for many was a daily factor in their business and family affairs.

The Diabo case allowed the Mohawks to travel freely across the U.S. border during the prosperous decade of the 1920s, but it also was used by some to rationalize the smuggling of alcohol from Canada during the Prohibition era. Using Akwesasne's geography, its open border (at least on the reservation itself), and the vast freshwater marshes in its eastern section, the Mohawks found it relatively easy to bring their cargo of beer, wine, and spirits across the St. Lawrence for delivery to American sources, who then arranged transport throughout the northeast.

The praxis could be lucrative, but it had its risks. Payoffs had to be made to the American border patrol and state police, or a smuggler risked confiscation of his goods and arrest followed by a prison term in grim facilities such as nearby Dannemora or distant Atlanta. Stories are told of Mohawks being executed for failing to pay the required bribes, their bodies found weighted down beneath the cold St. Lawrence waters.

The 1920s were a time of increased political activism for all Iroquois. The remnant Oneidas scored an unexpected legal win when their claim to the last 32 acres of reservation land in their aboriginal territory was sustained by the U.S. Supreme Court. It wasn't much, but it gave them an opportunity to begin reconstruction of a viable Oneida community.

In 1924 the U.S. Congress enacted the American Indian Citizenship Act, a law which the Iroquois, as a whole, rejected. The leaders knew it would be impossible for the Haudenosaunee to sustain a formal treaty with the United States if they accepted citizenship in what they saw as an alien nation. They also held firm to the provisions of the Kaswenta, the Two Row Wampum, which forbade the Iroquois from leaving their canoes to cross into the boats of the Europeans. Kaswenta, an agreement between the Dutch and the Haudenosaunee, dates from the 1640's. As was the Haudenosaunee custom, the agreement was secured by having it made into a wampum belt consisting of purple and white quahog shell beads. The Haudenosaunee have sought to apply the principles of the agreement, prohibiting interference in each other's affairs, to each successive European-based government including the United States.

The Confederacy had also sought formal acknowledgment of its national status from the League of Nations. Levi General of Oshweken had been installed as a *rotiiane,* or chief, of the Cayugas with the title name Deskaheh. He was given the task of traveling to the headquarters of the League in Geneva, Switzerland, to press the Iroquois claims. While he managed to stimulate popular interest in Europe regarding Native issues, his actions incurred the wrath of the Canadian government, which denied him permission to return home. Exhausted and discouraged, Deskaheh died at the Tuscarora home of Clinton Rickard in 1925, but his sacrifices on behalf of the people set an example for generations of other Iroquois, Rickard being foremost.

Rickard created the Indian Defense League of America in 1927. The Defense League worked to protect Native rights. Rickard adhered to the example set by Deskaheh, devoting the rest of his life to the principle that the Iroquois were an independent people. He, in turn, heavily influenced a young Mohawk teacher named Ray Fadden, who, in turn, would completely change the culture and politics of the Mohawk Nation.

Fadden, as will be detailed in chapter 3, brought his form of activism right into the classroom. His students would form the core of a new wave of aboriginal leaders who would, in turn, cross the continent, encouraging Native youths to take direct charge of their communities.

First, Fadden had to work with a community struck hard by the Depression. The easy money made during Prohibition had ended with the repeal of the 18th Amendment in 1933, but tough times had already begun to affect the Mohawks. Many families abandoned the reservation during the winter months, retreating into the forests of northern New York and eastern Ontario, where they scraped by as lumberjacks and basket weavers.

In the spring they would return to the reservation after the ice had broken free from the rivers to cast their nets during the annual fish runs. Truck gardens were an essential part of insuring that enough food was put aside for the colder months since steady jobs were either seasonal or simply too hard to get, particularly when most Mohawks received only a few short years of formal education before being taken out of school to add their labor to the family's meager resources.

Mohawk men ventured hundreds of miles from home to search for jobs as ironworkers, an occupation they had easily mastered a generation before. From Seattle to New York they were a part of the massive public works projects sponsored by the Roosevelt administration, but their pay was not enough to lift the community out of poverty. It would take a world war to do that.

As they had in all previous American conflicts, the Mohawks eagerly enlisted in the armed forces after war was declared in 1941. Virtually every young Mohawk adult enlisted in either the U.S. or Canadian military. They proved to be adept soldiers and sailors, none more so than the former students of Ray Fadden. He had formed a Boy Scout troop, which later developed into the Akwesasne Mohawk Counselor Organization. The membership was made up of boys and girls who were taught Iroquois woodcraft such as tracking and wilderness survival. Fadden's students were physically healthy, self-reliant, and accustomed to working in small groups, all of which proved to be ideal skills in combat situations.

Akwesasne's soldiers fought with distinction in Europe, Asia, and Africa. They were part of U.S. General George Patton's Third Army as it rumbled toward the Rhine River or served in the Canadian Third Army when it landed at Normandy on D-Day, June 6, 1944. They endured the December cold at Bastogne, then liberated German concentration camps at the war's end.

Upon their return the servicemen found new opportunities for work in an expanding economy. The war industries had attracted many Mohawk women to cities such as Syracuse, Rochester, and Buffalo, where they were followed by the former servicemen. Entire families were uprooted from the reservation for new lives in an urban environment. Within a generation the majority of the Iroquois, including the Mohawks, would live away from their ancestral homes, primarily in or near a large American city.

The movement toward unification at Akwesasne was not deterred by the war. The passage of the Indian Reorganization Act of 1934 loosened the grip the U.S. federal government had over the administration of Native affairs. Indian communities were given the option of selecting how they were to be governed: traditional or elective. The residents of the American side chose in 1935, 1938, and again in 1948 to reject the New York State–empowered three-trustee system and to revive the clan system. At each instance, State officials acted to return the trustees to power, using its state police to conduct elections off the reservation.

The St. Regis Tribal Council was retained because the U.S. federal government and New York State had development plans that would affect Akwesasne.

Large aluminum smelting plants, an essential element of the war and post-war economies, were built adjacent to the reservation. The construction of the St. Lawrence Seaway, beginning in 1954, required the widening of the St. Lawrence River channel to enable ocean vessels to carry their cargo to and from the continental interior. Along with the various dams came the massive St. Lawrence Power Dam located on the north shore of Barnhart Island, immediately to the west of Akwesasne.

The power dam was on contested lands, with the Mohawks claiming their title had never been extinguished, but that they had lost active possession of Barnhart when the international border was redrawn north of the island after the War of 1812 and was affirmed in 1842.

Additional territory was set to be lopped off the reservation as the channel was widened, affecting property on Cornwall Island, Racquette Point, and several of the smaller islands on the Canadian side. Protest and litigation proved futile as the American courts proved particularly hostile to the idea that an aboriginal land claim could delay or stop one of the largest national public works projects in American history.

Tempering the loss suffered in the courts was the lure of hundreds of construction and ironworking jobs as well as the possibility of permanent employment in the nearby factories. Material prosperity was realized, but not before the traditional lifestyle of the Mohawks had been permanently altered when the Seaway welcomed its first ships in the spring of 1959.

The damming of the St. Lawrence destroyed the fishing industry on the reservation by slowing the flow of the water, which in turn gave rise to an explosion in algae growth, obscuring the nesting grounds of the fish. The airborne emissions from the industrial plants in Cornwall and Massena crippled the farm animals on the reservation and coated crops with an unhealthy residue of polychlorinated biphenyls (PCBs), a known carcinogen. The water discharges from factories were absorbed by the fish, which in turn made those who ate them likely to ingest dangerous levels of mercury, mirex, and many other harmful chemicals.

The radical changes in the air, land, and water compelled the Mohawks to find other means to live. The majority of male adult wage earners entered the ironworking trade, while Mohawk women took advantage of liberal education programs to secure college degrees. For the first time in many generations the Akwesasne community was receiving adequate medical care, leading to an explosion in the reservation population. The total number of Mohawks doubled from World War II to the 1960s and doubled again a generation later.

Operating large farms was not possible given the high demand for housing. The hayfields and cow pastures were converted into single-family lots, upon which homes designed by federal agencies rose by the hundreds.

Formal education became a priority of the Mohawk leadership. New schools were built and the older ones torn down to make way for hundreds of students. The ancient land-based teachings were pushed aside as irrelevant, as was the Mohawk language itself since it had little meaning in a cash-based society. Beginning in the early 1950s and coinciding with the Seaway and the introduction of television, the Mohawk language began to ebb from family homes. Indigenous knowledge which was thousands of years old and which could only be expressed in Mohawk was at risk of being fatally compromised.

The accelerating rate of acculturation was countered by the rise in popular support for the longhouse spiritual practices and the advent of a new generation of Native activism, stimulated in large part among the Mohawks by the fear that they were losing the most essential parts of their aboriginal heritage.

As they traveled throughout America, the Mohawks were aware of the rise in the civil rights movement. Mohawks were veracious readers of newspapers, which, alongside the broadcast mediums of television and radio, kept them informed as to the struggles by black Americans to rid themselves of the last vestiges of slavery. The Mohawk experiences in the military and their contact with other Native people in the construction trades enabled them to share their own experiences while coming to the conclusion that their own struggles to retain their status as a distinct people would be best served by taking an active role in a national movement.

The longhouse leadership proved to be flexible in this regard. Its council members had endured considerable personal risk and ridicule as they sought to practice their pagan ceremonies. While the traditional governmental elements had been retained, in part with the support of the Catholic Church, those who sought to restore the longhouse at Akwesasne could not muster sufficient internal support until the mid-1930s. Once the Indian Reorganization Act committed the U.S. federal government to permit a more aggressive exercising of Native self-determination, the longhouse adherents, those who were compelled to meet in small groups behind shuttered windows, felt strong enough to defy the church and build a longhouse in the center of the reservation on the American side.

The longhouse people directly assumed the governing mandate held by the longhairs, those who were the inheritors of the nine life chiefs. The Oswegatchie Iroquois added their three clan chiefs to the Mohawk nine, resulting in 12, a number which held until the longhouse returned to the former in the 1930s. The formal installation of chiefs, clanmothers, and faithkeepers in accordance with Haudenosaunee custom began at that time. The name titles of the chiefs were revived and the lunar-based ceremonies openly attended.

The contradictions that confronted the Akwesasne Mohawks at the beginning of the 1960s were intense, ongoing, and, for many, bewildering. Their former lifestyles were fading. Linguistic divisions between the pre- and postwar generations were growing. Adherence to the Christian faith was diminishing, yet the longhouse had grasped the support of a new group, called "teenagers." Mohawks now worked for money, not merely for a living. They were prosperous in the Western sense but were disturbed by the erosion in their treaty rights. Most families had eagerly embraced formal education just as they were being approached by dissatisfied middle class Americans, eager to find life's meaning within the traditional teachings of the Haudenosaunee.

Ray Fadden and community leaders such as Ernest Benedict, Alec Gray, Joe Mitchell, Ross David, Moses David, Ira Benedict, and Frank "Standing Arrow" Thomas sought to give resolve to those contradictions by advocating direct action. Standing Arrow gave the first push in this direction in 1954 when he led a group of Akwesasne and Kahnawake Mohawks back to their former, pre-Revolutionary War homes in the Mohawk Valley west of Albany, New York.

Their encampment on the west bank of Schoharie Creek, near Ft. Hunter, New York, lasted for two years, until they were removed by New York officials then overseeing the building of the State Thruway. When their longhouse was torched by the state police, the Mohawks returned home, vowing one day to return. The Mohawks maintained that their homelands had never been surrendered by any legitimate treaty and that they had rightful, historic claim to an aboriginal territory that stretched from the west branch of the Delaware River to the St. Lawrence and from Lake Champlain to the West Canada Creek near Herkimer, New York. In land area, this amounted to over nine million acres in New York State alone.

The longhouse people, as represented by the Mohawk Nation Council of Chiefs, did not take part in the failed land claims litigation of the St. Regis Tribal Council during the 1950s. They would not be drawn into hostile courts, but the leaders realized as a result of the Standing Arrow experience that direct assertion of an aboriginal right was preferable to the courts for even if an occupation was unsuccessful in the short run, the attendant publicity enhanced their standing both within their own community and around the nation.

The longhouse people did things to protect Mohawk rights, while the other two "elected" councils were obsessed with federal, provincial, and state-funded programs, making it far less likely that they would engage in any act which threatened their operating budgets. Being money poor, the Mohawk Nation was unencumbered by this problem and without such a qualification was free to challenge the prevailing system and press aggressively for the creation of a nation state based on aboriginal principles.

By 1968, a group of young Mohawks, heavily influenced by Standing Arrow and the civil rights movement, was ready to take on tribal, band, state, provincial, and federal authorities. Realizing the power of the media, they secured a film crew from the National Film Board of Canada, and on December 6, 1968, they stopped all traffic crossing the Seaway International Bridges, both spans of which were anchored on the Cornwall Island section of the reservation.

The event, as designed, attracted universal coverage from the media. But the organizers of the blockade went one step further: they elected to cut and paste the news clippings from the world press, compile them into a single journal, and thereby create their own newspaper. To market this publication, called *Akwesasne Notes,* they would adopt a strategy from the Unity caravans organized in part by the Tuscarora leader Wallace "Mad Bear" Anderson and the cultural excursions led by Ray Fadden. The Unity trips were loosely organized by the Haudenosaunee as a way to visit troubled spots and to share information among the native nations. There was a strong spiritual component to the trips as the various participants recited prayers, made offerings of tobacco at sacred sites, and shared songs and dances. The caravans crisscrossed the continent for most of the 1960s.

The plan was to create a mobile teaching group called the White Roots of Peace, which would bypass the media altogether and travel directly to Indian reservations, urban centers, prisons, and educational facilities. The members of the travel troupe would be schooled in Native activism and would teach others how to organize on the community level. They would advocate for the revival of traditional ways and encourage the direct application of Indian sovereignty as interpreted according to indigenous law and not those of Canada or the United States.

The White Roots of Peace would carry not only publications such as *Akwesasne Notes,* the most radically nationalistic of all Native journals, but books, posters, and artwork from throughout the Americas. It would provide entertainment in the way of Native folk singers and traditional dancers. For one reasonable price a college could book the entire troupe and have Native speakers address classes free from secondary interpreters, buy books from Native authors, or take part in a Mohawk-style social dance.

The White Roots formula succeeded in lighting the fires of Native nationalism wherever it went. Its actual membership was fluid and might include a Mayan from Guatemala, an Anishnabe from northern Ontario, an Inuit from the Northwest Territories, or Lakotas from the Great Plains. But its overall character was Mohawk, and for ten years it crisscrossed the United States and Canada, pressing Indians to stand in defiance of the mechanisms of oppression.

The traditional leaders among the Mohawks were advocates for peaceful change but soon came to realize their efforts to create change were being met with suspicion by investigative and governmental authorities in Canada and the United States. The Federal Bureau of Investigation (FBI) determined that Native political activism was cause for concern and began a program to infiltrate and destabilize the movement internally.

In some instances the activists were met with hostility from their own governments. The American Indian Movement (AIM), formed among urban-based Indians in 1968, was targeted as a disruptive force characterized by sensationalism and without regard to the long-term consequences of its actions. While many Mohawks supported AIM as individuals, it was never able to gain a foothold in Iroquois territory, primarily because of existing institutions which were able to internally direct regional acts of dissent and protest.

A key factor among the Iroquois youth was the adherence to the longhouse teachings and ceremonies, both of which formed the basis upon which they acted. But the rebirth of the warrior societies was not to be dissuaded or denied. Many Mohawks were convinced that peaceful protest was not enough. They reasoned that armed resistance would be the best means of defending Indian communities against unwarranted intrusions. A few months after the Wounded Knee, South Dakota, standoff ended in the spring of 1973, the newly formed "warrior society" at Kahnawake decided to evict non-Natives from their territory. Some of them were present at Onondaga in 1971 when the New York State Police were ordered to invade the Iroquois capital when its residents stopped an expansion of Interstate 81 through the northeast section of the reservation. At the last moment the troopers, heavily armed and keyed for a battle with equally armed Iroquois, were sent to quell the riot at the Attica State Prison. The bullets meant for the people at Onondaga were used against the Attica inmates, but the State did concede to the Native demands with regards to the highway.

The leaders of the warriors at Kahnawake felt their willingness to use force to effect their demands would also work. In October they began the evictions, with a predictable response from Quebec officials. Its provincial police were sent in, met with counterforce, and were compelled to retreat when they discovered the warriors had been organized into an effective defensive force by AIM veterans from Wounded Knee.

The warriors were stimulated by their moral victory, which led their leaders to consider another bold plan, one born twenty years before in the Mohawk Valley. They would assert their status as Mohawks not by seeking approval from the courts or formal recognition by either federal government, but through direct action. In the spring of 1974 they, in conjunction with a small Akwesasne contingent, picked up their weapons and drove to a Girl Scout camp near Eagle Bay, New York, in the western Adirondacks.

Named after a small lake, the encampment at Moss Lake was sustained for three years, primarily by Mohawks armed and willing to take on whatever force New York threw against it. Locals disliked the Mohawk occupation, and shots were fired into the camp, whose defenders returned fire, resulting in the wounding of a young non-Native girl. Tensions were very high, with demands the state police intervene to arrest the Mohawks. New York's Secretary of State was a young lawyer named Mario Cuomo, who believed there was an alternative to the impending war. He met with the leaders of Ganienkeh, the Mohawk term for the encampment, and convinced them to move closer to the Canadian border, on state-owned property 15 miles west of Plattsburgh.

In 1977, the Moss Lake occupiers left that region, but they had proven an important point that came to characterize Iroquois politics for the next generation, namely, that the application of direct action backed up by the threat of force will inevitably compel non-Native governments to make critical concessions with regard to the exercise of aboriginal sovereignty.

At Akwesasne, officials with the St. Regis Tribe were beginning to expand their existing services but required formal recognition from the U.S. federal government to qualify for grants. In 1972, they were given a letter from Bureau of Indian Affairs director Louis Bruce, himself an Akwesasne Mohawk, stating that he personally acknowledged the tribe.

Armed with the Bruce letter, the Tribe sought to counter the longhouse activities, which they feared would lead to demands for the dismantling of the Tribal Council in favor of traditional government. The very low turnouts at the annual tribal elections were indicative of lukewarm support for the elected system among the American-based Mohawks, but it was sufficient for it to lay claim to being the only Mohawk council with formal U.S. and New York State standing.

The Tribe took advantage of readily available federal policing funds and created its own tribal police, who were empowered to enforce state laws on Indian territory, an extension of the criminal and civil jurisdiction cessions made by the United States to New York in 1948 and 1952. For the longhouse people, this extension of state jurisdiction was an unwarranted intrusion into the community and had to be opposed. Communications between the Tribe and the Mohawk Nation Council were virtually nonexistent, resulting in misunderstandings and mutual suspicion. Since the tribal police had no formal training in traditional laws or arbitration techniques, conflict was inevitable.

The Tribe attempted, in 1973, to evict a couple of longhouse families from their homes on the American side, claiming they were Canadian Mohawks without proper enrollment status. Forced to back down when confronted by a large group of protesters, the Tribe tried again in May 1979 to enforce its jurisdictional claims when it sent a work crew to clear brush on the western edge of the reservation. They were met by a longhouse member who ordered them off what he claimed was his property. The Tribal police were called in to retrieve equipment that had been confiscated but were soon involved in a struggle that led to minor physical injuries and arrests of longhouse people.

The response from the Mohawk Nation was swift as the incident provided its supporters with an opportunity to challenge the Tribe collectively. A large procession composed of hundreds of longhouse people marched from their ceremonial building in the center of the reservation to the offices of the Tribal Council a mile away. Once they got there they were met by the Tribal police, who refused a demand that they resign. Frustrated by their stance and the collapse of an earlier negotiating session, the leadership turned away from the police and gave the matter over to the people. With a Tyendinaga Mohawk leading the charge, dozens of Mohawk men rushed toward the police, grabbing their arms, stripping them of their handguns, and pushing them out of their headquarters.

Tribal officials were caught off guard but in the following hours rallied their supporters, many of whom were heavily armed. The standoff was diffused for the moment when the longhouse people agreed to leave the police headquarters, but not before stripping the office of all its weapons.

Criminal indictments were issued by the local county's grand jury as a result of the incident, which compelled the Mohawk Nation to organize an encampment at the Racquette Point district of Akwesasne. A massive state police strike in August

1979 resulted in the arrests of three longhouse individuals and forced the Nation to prepare for an Attica-style attack.

The assault never came, although there were instances when the Tribe and longhouse came perilously close to using their guns. On June 13, 1980, the Nation received word that the troopers were set to enter the camp when dozens of tribal and state cops sealed off the reservation. That attack evaporated when the other members of the Haudenosaunee Confederacy banded together to inform New York Governor Hugh Carey that should the troopers fire upon the Mohawks, the power and gas lines that ran through the various Iroquois communities would be cut. In addition, every state and federal highway built on Indian land would be blockaded.

Since the state police had no formal training in controlling a massive uprising, Governor Carey would have had to use the National Guard. The resultant escalation would have placed thousands of state residents in jeopardy as electrical power would have been terminated to hospitals, schools, and private residences. Carey ordered the troopers to retreat, a decision that once again confirmed the belief held by many Mohawks that New York would do anything to avoid having to fight with well-armed Iroquois.

That perception would have terrible ramifications at Akwesasne in 1990, when the warrior proponents used this tactic against their own people.

CHAPTER 3

Ray Fadden-Tehanetorens

The month of August is called Seskeha in Mohawk, the moon of freshness, when life is at its peak and the bean, corn, and squash crops are ready for harvest.

It is also the time to return to the Adirondacks, the ancient hunting and gathering ground of the Haudenosaunee and particularly the Mohawks, whose aboriginal territory includes the entire range of mountains between the St. Lawrence valley and the Mohawk River.

The Adirondacks were a common hunting preserve whose resources were open to all Native people, provided they abided by a few simple rules, primarily ones aimed at preservation. Rule one was this: take only what you need, and use all that you take.

Haudenosaunee hunters were highly trained from their youth to track, kill, clean, and preserve game, from birds to the largest mammals. Nothing was left to chance or speculation when a boy was given his first hunting tools. He not only spent days perfecting his shooting skills with bow and arrow, but he was taught which trees made the best bows and how to make his own flint-tipped projectiles.

Boys were shown the proper way to hurl a spear or use a blowgun. They were carefully instructed as to the movement of the animals they were tracking and where to strike when the target presented itself. Endurance was emphasized since the hunt would require hiking through miles of heavily forested land or canoeing upstream, against the flow of fast-moving rivers and streams.

From how to make a fire in a rainstorm to which organ of a fresh kill provided the greatest source of immediate energy, the Haudenosaunee boy developed into a young man at ease with his environment and capable of extraordinary feats of physical strength. He was taught about trees and herbs, how to cure scurvy or set a broken bone, all essential skills when a wounded man was without recourse to an emergency room.

By the time the youth had become a man, he was without equal in wood-craft and knowledge of his environment. He was also a custodian of the resources that he used to perpetuate his life and that of his community for the Haudenosaunee were careful to add a spiritual element to their teachings. All hunters had clan affiliations, and all clans had an animal totem, along with personal and clan names taken directly from nature.

As an example, a member of the Wolf Clan with the name "Skywalker" would develop an appreciation for the species to which he belonged. He would be less inclined to see the wolf as removed from himself and would learn all he could about the habits of the animal, perhaps even incorporating some elements of the wolf into his own personal life. So, too, his name.

Among the Mohawks, there are three clans: Bear, Wolf, and Turtle. Children are instructed to be sensitive to the needs of the clan animal to which they belong and to make sure such creatures are as healthy and vigorous as they are. Attached to the clans are permanent sets of names that are handed down from one generation to the next. When a person dies, his name returns to the clan to be given to a newborn at one of the main lunar ceremonies, primarily Midwinter, in mid- or late January.

A person may be recognized as to their clan by his individual name. Those of the Bear Clan will have names that are of the forest, trees, or plants for that is the world of the bear animal. A Wolf Clan member will have a name that reflects the sky world since wolves like to look to the heavens and sing to the skies. A Turtle Clan person is naturally of the water, and hence his name will reflect rivers, water plants, or ice.

All these factors were summarized in a singular belief common to all Haudenosaunee, namely, that which exists has spirit, and that which has spirit must be addressed in thought, prayer, and action. With this cardinal rule the Haudenosaunee developed a culture which was distinct in that it enabled humans to physically prosper without inflicting harm on the natural world.

This was certainly true of the Adirondacks, a region called Tsonontiskowa ("the great mountains") in Mohawk. Well into the twentieth century, the Mohawk people retained an intimate knowledge of the Adirondacks, a legacy from their ancestors who knew of every stream, mountain, or valley within its six million acres, a familiarity developed over hundreds of years.

Knowledge was awareness, and awareness was simple common sense to the Mohawks. Those who came before us built their main communities to the south and north of the mountains for trade, planting, and comfort purposes. They avoided the bogs and still ponds of the mountain region during the late spring and early summer months as the blackflies, deerflies, and mosquitoes made life close to unbearable. By late July and early August, most of the flies had disappeared, their short lives having run their course. Mohawks would then return to gather berries, pick herbal medicines, and harvest sweetgrass for use in baskets and as an air and home purifier.

The old way of entering the mountains was by water. The Racquette was a particularly favored route used by the St. Lawrence River–based Mohawks, while the Hudson River provided entry from the south, as did the West Canada Creek to the southwest. Later, logging companies would make use of the region's many rivers to float timber from the mountains to distant sawmills, where the boards could be loaded into barges for delivery to markets in Montreal or New York.

As formidable as the Mohawk reputation was in warfare or, later, as high steel ironworkers, they were also known, and respected, for their skills with a steel ax and their willingness to guide massive flotillas of logs through river rapids to the mills. Their quick feet, marked by toes which pointed slightly inward, enabled the Mohawk lumberjacks to dance across the logs and shimmy quickly up to the peaks of the tallest white pines.

There was another sound reason why the Mohawks began to leave their homes during Seskeha month. Since much of the crops would be harvested in weeks leading up to the first frost, but a few short weeks away, they would search for jobs to carry them through the cold months in areas where they had sufficient firewood to heat their cabins.

By the end of the nineteenth century, most of Akwesasne had been stripped bare of large trees. The Mohawks could not relocate their community as in former days, and neither woods or land were able to fully recover from years of cutting and planting on the reservation. Since wood was the only heat source used by Mohawk households, they had to find accommodation where there were sufficient trees, which meant many Mohawk families closed their drafty reservation homes to find shelter, jobs, and heat in the forests of Ontario or the Adirondacks.

The men were hired as lumberjacks, the wives as cooks. They labored hard during the short winter days, and in the evenings they bent beneath flickering kerosene lamps to weave sweetgrass and black ash splint baskets for sale by the dozen to tourists and collectors during the spring and summer. Once the spring came, with the breaking of the ice and the booming of the logs across the rapids, the Mohawks returned to their reservation homes.

The Mohawk families would leave Akwesasne on horse-drawn buckboard wagons to be carried to the railroad station in the northern New York hamlet of Helena, where they would board for the long ride into the Adirondacks. Trains would stop at the various logging camps to discharge passengers loaded with their tools and clothing.

Railway lines followed the old trails and riverbanks into the heart of the mountains. It was easy for the Mohawks to recognize where they were at any given time. They knew certain wetlands were particularly good places to gather sweetgrass or a specific herb used to cure sickness. By the twentieth century, most of the larger mammals had been exterminated from the Adirondacks, including the beloved wolf, but the old hunting grounds were not forgotten.

After the last great harvesting of trees in the Adirondacks had taken place during the Great Depression, the Mohawks were not seen in the mountains as frequently as before. The railway lines were abandoned by the logging companies as there were few virgin strands of trees left to cut. The rails were ripped up, as were the ties upon which they had lain. But the rail beds remained, and it was along these routes the Mohawks hiked to return to their former harvest and hunting grounds.

Seskeha month was not only the best time to return to the Adirondacks for berry picking, but it was also the ideal time to visit with the legendary Ray Fadden of the Six Nations Indian Museum in the tiny village of Onchiota, 15 miles north of the town of Saranac Lake, in a region that had the oldest of mountains in all of northern New York.

Ray Fadden was as much a part of the natural history of the area as the bears and trees. He was the ideal blend of determined Scotch and freedom-loving Mohawk ancestry, two peoples who had forged a mutual admiration and attraction long before the American Revolution. When the Scots were driven from their Mohawk Valley homes during that war, they found refuge with their Mohawk allies in eastern Ontario and later moved into the Adirondacks.

Fadden carried the Mohawk name Tehanetorens from the Wolf Clan, and like that animal, he was independent, loyal to his people, and fierce in the protection of his family and beliefs. He was born in August (naturally) 1910, a few miles west of Onchiota, in a region in which his family had lived for generations. A teacher by training, he obtained his degree from the Fredonia Normal School (now the State University of New York at Fredonia), southwest of Buffalo. From there he secured a job at the reservation school at Tuscarora.

Fadden loved his students, as did they him. He was influenced by the life-long efforts of the Tuscarora leader Clinton Rickard, an ardent, outspoken advocate for the Haudenosaunee throughout most of the twentieth century. When others had reached the point of giving up their Iroquois heritage and treaty status, Rickard took a stance against those fatal compromises. He was a part of a remarkable group of Iroquois nationalists that included Mary Cornelius Winder, Levi General, Laura Cornelius Kellogg, Jesse Cornplanter, and Alice Lee Jemison, all of whom waged lifelong battles to not only preserve the essence of their heritage as Iroquois, but to seek justice for the lands and rights which had been stripped from the Haudenosaunee by New York and the U.S. federal government.

There was not much in the way of positive judicial rulings or a favorable political climate to give any of the activists hope they would be treated fairly in Congress or before the federal courts. Yet they would not let go of their common assertion that the Haudenosaunee were, and by international standards ought to be, independent entities with the inherent right to govern their own affairs while seeking redress for the theft of their aboriginal homelands.

Most of the Iroquois were not of the same passion. But Ray Fadden was. He would never concede his core principles to any individual or institution. He believed the Iroquois were not primitive in thought, technology, or belief. His ancestors were complex, sophisticated, and politically enlightened far beyond what was taught in the school texts.

Fadden elected to carry the passion of the Iroquois nationalists into the very system that had tried to shatter Haudenosaunee pride: the schools. He began with a simple idea—the key to liberating the enormous intellectual and physical talents of Iroquois boys and girls was to speak the truth as to their history and convince them that such truth had merit and could be found within the stories of their own families.

Teaching Iroquois students to be proud rather than submissive was revolutionary and to do so within the reservation schools outright heresy. But Fadden found support not only from the children, but from the parents as well. While many were defensive about their culture and had been told the "old ways" were to be discarded if the children were to survive in a changed world, Fadden's students found adults who were proud of what they were and eager to share their knowledge with the younger generation.

Fadden's methods were highly effective. He revealed for his students a world that the schools and churches had done their best to obscure. When he decided to leave Tuscarora in 1938 to return to the Akwesasne region, he left behind an enduring legacy of honesty, integrity, and enthusiasm that the Tuscarora people would not forget.

Fadden followed his Mohawk roots back home, where he and his wife Christine were welcomed. His decision to take a job teaching grade five at the St. Regis Mohawk School on the U.S. side of the reservation gave him the opportunity to press ahead with his innovative curriculum. He and his students spent years researching Mohawk history in areas most so-called scholars had ignored. They placed great emphasis on the oral traditions and teachings of the Haudenosaunee since they knew their elders would not lie about any event or a cultural practice or belief.

The students learned the true origins of the Iroquois, which was not in Asia, but in the continental southwest. They came to realize that the only true democracy in the world was practiced not in Europe, but was an invention from the minds of the Native people. They discovered that most of the food that was consumed by the earth's peoples was developed by Native scientists and that their ancestors were mathematicians, architects, philosophers, biologists, physicians, and astronomers, in addition to being soldiers, hunters, and artists.

Fadden had the students create a series of charts which, for the first time anywhere, showed the enormous contributions Native people made to humanity and how current events were profoundly shaped by these gifts. From rubber to quinine and chocolate to cotton it was the Native creative genius that clothed the world's nations and enhanced their diets, thereby enabling people to live longer and in better health.

Fadden had them look back into the primary records when Europeans and Natives first met. They were surprised by the differences in height and physique between the two peoples, with the Native adult being much taller and far stronger than the colonist. This was no accident, Fadden taught, but a direct result of superior diet, a culture that stressed exercise, better medical care, and a mental outlook in which the individual was free from the restrictions of class or artificial privilege.

Particularly intriguing for the Mohawks was the role of women in traditional Iroquois society. They were not chattel or appendages to men, but were free to take part in the public affairs of their nations while enjoying liberty to go about as they pleased. It was the women who nominated all leaders and impeached them for misconduct. Iroquois women held the economic reigns of the nation since they determined how resources were to be allocated, from land to food distribution. While women in European society were legally children, or even less, the Iroquois woman helped forge a culture in which she enjoyed the highest standard of freedom anywhere in the world.

Fadden directed the attention of the students to other areas, particularly the environment. He knew the Mohawks were a generous and kind people with a high degree of sensitivity toward the rights of other species. Fadden elected to emphasize this part of his teaching by creating the Akwesasne Mohawk Counselor Organization, a group that stressed woodcraft, art, and history from a uniquely Iroquois perspective.

The appeal of the group to teenage kids was like rain in the desert. Fadden's kids would revive the ancient methods of learning by observing the work of their elders and then applying it to whatever task was at hand. They were at ease during their frequent trips into the Adirondacks, where they sat around the campfire listening to Fadden tell stories of long ago.

Fadden also introduced the boys and girls to Iroquois music. They were able to hear the remarkable songs of Jesse Cornplanter, the Seneca master who could recite hundreds of verses of chants from dozens of different songs. They also were able to learn from Arthur C. Parker, the Seneca anthropologist and historian who had spent a lifetime researching Iroquois history and culture.

Fadden took his students on long trips throughout the east to visit different Native communities and historical sites. His arrival caused excitement among his hosts for here was a group which actually promoted a positive image of indigenous people.

Fadden also had the courage to stand strong against the forces of discrimination and prejudice within the Akwesasne Mohawk community. Many Mohawks did not like his methods since they placed organized Christianity in a critical light.

The Jesuits had a mission at Akwesasne, one of its last in North America. The priests assigned to the St. Regis Mission were quick to learn the Mohawk language, which, along with Latin, were the only two forms of expression heard in the local Catholic Church during mass. The priest wielded great power over the community as most Mohawks were Catholic, and even those who were sympathetic to the traditional, or longhouse, ways found it safer to practice the pagan rituals at places far away, such as Onondaga or Oshweken.

The priest had a number of tactics for suppressing the pagan ceremonies. He could withhold communion from the offending family, reject their confessions, deny the deceased burial in consecrated grounds, or hold them up to public censure during mass. He could also apply pressure on the local Indian agent, an individual with dictatorial powers appointed by federal bureaucrats, or sway elections for the tribal and band councils on both sides of the border.

The priest also influenced social welfare, oversaw all birth, death, and marriage records, and taught catechism at the Mission school, which was located two miles north of Fadden's public school classroom.

Fadden did not hesitate to shake things up in the most profound way when he arrived at Akwesasne. He openly supported a small group of Mohawks who were ready to defy the Catholic Church and 200 years of history by building a longhouse on the reservation where they could openly, and with pride, conduct the 15 ceremonies which mark the traditional calendar, none of which had anything to do with Christianity.

The Jesuit priest in charge of the Mission at that time was a Mohawk, Michael Jacobs, from the Kahnawake community across the St. Lawrence River from Montreal. He was a powerful speaker, passionate, driven, and committed to the church. He met, in Ray Fadden, a person who would not back down from him, had no fear of being branded a pagan, and did not hesitate to expose the sordid history of the church with regards to its treatment of Native people.

Within a year of Fadden's arrival the longhouse was alive, and the long-dormant ceremonies were being held, to the wrath of Reverend Jacobs. The Akwesasne Mohawks had retained their language, traditional political structure, and many of the family-based customs that are an essential part of Haudenosaunee culture. What they did not have was a common place to revive the collective rituals for the community. For many decades Mohawks had taken part in the ancient ceremonies as held on different territories, but emboldened by the political activists of that era, the traditionalists, or longhouse practitioners went public.

The first few years were difficult. There were not many others willing to risk ridicule or security by entering the longhouse. While the adults were able to make use of a shifting political climate to exercise their religious rights, their children were subject to ridicule by their peers or exclusion at the Mission school.

In Fadden's class, there was no such doubt. He showed the students how to demonstrate their Mohawk pride by reviving the old style of dress. Up to that time, most Mohawks used Lakota war bonnets or Cheyenne leggings when they made any kind of public appearance, with the women clothed in fringed buckskin and beaded headbands. It would take Fadden a few years, but he gradually convinced the students to wear the Mohawk feathered head-dress called the *kastowah* and to use Iroquois leggings, moccasins, and shirts instead of borrowing from other nations. His advocacy resulted in the war bonnets being put away to be replaced by Iroquois-designed clothing.

Fadden took another creative step in his commitment to tell the truth about the Haudenosaunee, and particularly the Mohawks. In 1955, after 17 years living at Akwesasne, he decided to make a partial return home to his ancestral grounds at Onchiota. Using his own limited financial resources, he built an intellectual sanctuary for the Iroquois, a place to preserve important Iroquois artifacts as well as a center for others to learn about the area's first peoples. He would build his own museum, the first ever created by Native people for Native people.

Fadden and his students knew how bad most museums were whenever they elected to show anything Native. Whether it was the Smithsonian Institution's Museum of Natural History, with its war-crazed depiction of an Iroquois man holding a blood-dripping scalp high above his head, or the public display of sacred funerary objects in local historical societies, they all distorted the truth and perpetuated harmful stereotypes, which in turn were used to justify the extermination of millions of Native people.

These myths could not be allowed to stand unchallenged, so Fadden did something that has become a Mohawk practice: he created an alternative rather than suffer in silence. His facility, the Six Nations Indian Museum, would counter the racist trash the academics and museologists were feeding the public. He would take his charts, his pamphlets, his artifacts, and his artwork, place them in a four-room building, and take on all who dared to question the Iroquois version of reality.

Without government grants or assistance from any external source Fadden harvested timber from his Adirondack property and hauled the trees (after he had spoken words of gratitude to each one) to the mill, where they were made into boards. Fadden had the assistance of some of his students in raising the building and completing the interior (his main crew were Julius Cook, Art Einhorn, Frank Alexander, and Billy Loran, workers who asked for nothing other than to help Fadden realize his dream), but he labored with his son in the solitude of the surrounding forest for most of the time.

When the museum was completed in 1954, there was no particular cer-emony to mark its opening, yet it quickly became a powerful attraction for the Haudenosaunee, a place where they were greeted with enthusiasm by Ray and his son John-Kahionhes. After walking through the facility, with its floor-to-ceiling collection of artifacts, reading the wall charts composed by Mohawk students, or listening to one of Ray's powerful lectures about Native history, the Iroquois guest left feeling stronger, as if he had been renewed in mind and spirit.

In August, 1975, I had decided to make my own trek to the museum. Since I was a student at the St. Regis Village School, a Catholic facility whose teachers were nuns from the Sisters of St. Anne order, there was no chance of ever learning from Fadden in the classroom. Our school was over the international border on the Quebec side of the line. We were required to learn mathematics, grammar, and French, our handwriting was subject to close scrutiny, we mastered the basic elements of Catholicism, and we were rewarded for attending daily mass.

In the village's stone church, built in the 1790s by Mohawk craftsmen, including my own ancestors, we served as altar boys, a rank of honor among our peers. Since our home was across the street from the church, my brothers and I were naturally expected to take an active role in most church-related activities, whether it was ringing the steeple bell for vespers or letting the community know of the passing of a parishioner.

We also were told by our teachers of the depravity of the Iroquois and the cruelty of the Mohawks, in particular. Our heritage, prior to conversion, was one of violence, sensuality, warfare, and the vilest elements of paganism. We were historically tainted because our ancestors had burnt alive a number of Jesuit missionaries, and only by submission to the church were we saved from damnation.

The images of the Iroquois in the texts from which we learned were of demonic characters, their faces distorted by hate as they danced around a saintly priest affixed to an upright pole, his face looking toward the heavens as a large bundle of wood piled at his feet was about to be set afire. The agony of being burnt alive by savage Mohawks was temporized by the victim's belief that he would soon join Jesus Christ in a celestial paradise.

All of us were intimidated by the sacrifices of the North American martyrs. We came to know the priests Brebeuf, Lallemont, Jogues, Daniel, Garnier, and Chabenel, who, along with lay helpers Goupil and Lalande, died gloriously in the service of the church. Those men were our heroes, not, as Fadden would have wished, Iroquois leaders of stature, such as Theyanoguin Hendrick,

Aiionwatha, Deskaheh, Jikonsaseh, Skaniatariio, or Skennenrahowi, the great prophet of peace and founder of the Haudenosaunee Confederacy.

Fadden's teachings were forbidden fruit for Catholics on the Canadian side of Akwesasne. He had left the reservation school in 1957 to complete his teaching career at Saranac in 1967, but his legacy of defiance had great appeal to young Mohawks who had used their intellectual skills to question the world around them, including the church. I came to know him only after I had discarded Christianity to return to the longhouse but a short year before.

In the spring of 1975 I completed a tour with the White Roots of Peace. For me, taking part in the White Roots was enlightening, but it led back to the Six Nations Museum for inspiration. Ray Fadden's commitment to reviving the spirits of his Mohawk and Tuscarora students had reached far beyond the walls of the schools in which he had taught, and those of us involved in advancing indigenous causes were merely carrying on his work.

Like many others before me, I sat inside the small building listening to the harsh cries of the ravens. Fadden had created an animal sanctuary on his property and fed hundreds of birds as well as a few lumbering bears each day. He refused to allow any animal to be killed by so-called sportsmen. He lived in a simple home across the road from the museum but during its summer hours would arrive each and every day to give a lecture using his students' charts.

There was no better way to spend an August day in the northern Adirondacks than to listen to this articulate patriot tear at the lies and myths used by the Europeans to annihilate indigenous people and defile what had been a pristine land. I realized then that whatever truth I knew about the people I came from had been preserved against great odds by the convictions of one human being.

It was strange, I thought then, how thousands of years of experiences and learning could have come so close to extinction but for one person in a public school classroom and a simple museum in the deep, green mountains of the weathered Adirondacks. If ever there was a land in which to preserve Haudenosaunee history, Ray Fadden's Six Nations Museum was surely that place.

Equally intriguing was the callous manner in which some Mohawks would pervert Fadden's teachings, using his emphasis on national initiative, cultural affirmation, and indigenous sovereignty as the basis for gambling, smuggling, and narcotic trafficking.

CHAPTER 4

Land Claims

In the spring of 1984 I was asked by the Mohawk Nation Council of Chiefs to serve as part of the land claims negotiating team. The Nation had elected to become involved in the claims process as one of the three Native governing entities at Akwesasne and the only administration that had historical continuity since the time of the community's founding 240 years before. The ultimate goal of a land claims settlement was to create a contemporary aboriginal nation astride the St. Lawrence River, with complete and exclusive jurisdiction over its historical territories.

Five years before, in 1979, the Mohawk Nation Council was made aware of secret negotiations taking place between the St. Regis Tribal Council and New York State officials aimed at terminating the Mohawk claims to land lost to the original reservation as defined in 1796. The State offered a settlement package amounting to about $12 million in compensation, but without consulting with the Mohawk Nation Council or the Canadian-based Mohawk Council of Akwesasne (called the St. Regis Band Council).

The reaction of the supporters of the Mohawk Nation was swift. They condemned the actions of the Tribal Council as deceptive and unacceptable given the value of the disputed territory. The agreement needed the approval of a majority of the three-person Tribal Council to go into effect, but an incident involving the tribal police and a member of the Nation Council erupted into a confrontation between the factions which delayed, and then suspended, that phase of the claims discussions.

Tensions had already been rising on the reservation stemming from the reluctance of the traditional faction to recognize the policing authority of the Tribe, particularly when it used U.S. federal funds to create its police department, which sought to enforce New York State laws on Indian lands. This was, according to the longhouse people, a clear violation of Mohawk laws and a breach of the formal treaty relationship the Iroquois have with the United States. The Native rights movement begun a decade previous was rooted in part in Akwesasne, where the assertion of self-governing powers had been seriously impeded by the division of the reservation in half by the international border and the presence of two distinctly non-Mohawk governmental entities: the Tribal Council and its Canadian equivalent, the Band Council.

As the Mohawk Nation Council expanded its base of support, the administrative claims of the Tribe, in particular, were subject to frequent challenges by individuals who were longhouse members. There were occasional car chases and alleged police beatings, which increased tensions on the reservation. The successful land reclamation actions of the Ganienkeh movement demonstrated to the Iroquois that if confronted with an armed group of Natives, New York State would retreat from its efforts to apply its laws on Indian territory. When the St. Regis tribal police roughed up an assistant, or subchief, of the Nation Council for throwing a brush clearing crew off of the Raquette Point district of Akwesasne, the reaction by the traditional people was immediate.

A series of public meetings was held, during which the tribal police, in May of 1979, were invited to explain their actions before the people. They made one appearance, during which they were asked to resign their positions since their authority was vested with New York State and not with the Nation. When they refused to surrender their badges, the Mohawk people decided to walk from the longhouse to the Tribal Council offices, about one kilometer west, and demand the disbanding of the police. The procession consisted of hundreds of people from Akwesasne and other Mohawk communities present to observe the event and express their support for the Nation. The march was led by the leaders of the Mohawk Nation Council, followed by elders, women, a few children, and the men. Once they arrived at the heavily guarded Tribal complex, the Nation chiefs walked up to the police and once again asked them to resign. When they refused, the chiefs turned the matter over to the Mohawk men, who, after a few moments' hesitation, went as a group to the officers, stripped them of their side arms, and occupied not only their headquarters, but also the Tribe's main offices.

My task, as a young man, was to first assist in the disarming of the police, then to collect and inventory all of their weapons. Others were posted at various points in the building, while some examined the records of the Tribe. It was through these searches that the land claims negotiations were uncovered. The building was evacuated some hours later when Tribal supporters threatened to open fire at the occupiers. Warrants were issued against those who had taken part in the clash, but rather than face arrest, the longhouse people set up an armed encampment at Raquette Point to protect its leaders. A massive police strike by State and U.S. federal agents in August of that year resulted in the arrest of many individuals, including myself. We were held for 10 days in the nearby Franklin County jail in Malone, New York, before securing release on bail. Joining our legal team was the late William Kunstler, the noted civil rights attorney and founder of the Center for Constitutional Rights in New York. While charges against us were dismissed in the fall of that year, the Racquette Point camp would continue for over 18 months.

There were two tangible results arising from the 1979 incident. The first was the rejection of the proposed 1979 land claims agreement, with the second being the creation of the Akwesasne Freedom School, an education facility formed under the authority of the Mohawk Nation Council which stressed Native-based learning in a complete Mohawk language immersion curriculum. The Freedom School was part of a movement by the Iroquois to gain control over local schools. When the learning methods in those institutions proved to be unsatisfactory, the Mohawks of Kahnawake and Akwesasne decided to design their own, with a unique stress on language retention and traditional culture. The intent was to instill in the students a strong sense of pride in their heritage while changing the rate at which Mohawk children were being assimilated into Western society. The result was the aggressive assertion of aboriginal cultural, economic, and political rights by the Mohawk people.

The retreat from the brink of civil war in 1979–1980 initiated a new direction in Akwesasne's political life. The longhouse people took a more direct interest in the daily activities of the Tribal Council and managed to elect individuals who were supportive of its goals. The tribal police were dismantled by popular referendum in 1982 after Julius Cook, a respected war veteran, retired ironworker, and community leader, was swept into office in 1981. Cook's tenure was characterized by a high degree of cooperation among all three Mohawk councils. His unifying efforts were duplicated in 1984 when the electors on the Canadian side put into power a new 12-member council, which was also committed to working toward the resolution of issues common to all Akwesasne Mohawks.

The selection of a joint Mohawk land claims negotiating team came as a surprise to New York State. At the first session between the united Mohawk team and New York in April of 1984 the State expressed its hope that there would be a quick resolution of the issue. Joining our group were observers from the Onondaga Nation since we were in their aboriginal territory and our ancestral protocol mandated their participation. On the State's side of the table were representatives of the U.S. federal government since we had learned the perils of dealing with Albany alone.

After the recitation of the Ohenten Kariwatekwen, the traditional prayer of thanksgiving and humility spoken prior to all social, political, and spiritual gatherings of the Iroquois, the meeting began with New York State explaining its concern over the pending litigation without acknowledging its responsibility for taking Mohawk lands in violation of U.S. federal law. Our side responded with a polite summary of our concerns and the need for additional lands in anticipation of a rapid growth in our population. When it was appropriate, I spoke of the two pending Mohawk land claims, which caused the State representatives to react with puzzlement and suspicion.

The first claim, I said, arose over the State's taking of our land from the boundaries of the original reservation as defined in 1796 in a so-called Treaty with the Seven Nations of Canada, which was not binding on the Mohawk Nation since it never mentioned the Nation specifically. That "treaty" merely extinguished the nonexistent land claims of a loose alliance of Catholic Indian communities along the St. Lawrence River, which, in fact, transgressed upon the aboriginal lands of the Mohawks. The Akwesasne delegation disputed that treaty, which had set reservation lands at about 27,000 acres south of the international border. The specific areas cited as having been taken were in the towns of Massena and Ft. Covington, fields on either side of the Grasse River, and a wedge-shaped section in the center of the reservation referred to as Hogansburg.

While those sections had some value given the depleted soils and loss of forests, they were marginal at best for farming, trapping, or timber harvesting. The St. Lawrence islands, and in particular, Barnhart, were far more valuable to the State since the massive St. Lawrence Power Dam was located there. We were prepared to challenge the relicensing of the Power Authority of New York, the facility's operator, as a permanent source of income and free electricity for all of Akwesasne.

The second claim would come after we had resolved the first. That one would be for the 9.9 million acres lost by us after the American Revolution. When I brought this matter to the table, the State responded by saying that the resolution of the smaller claim meant all Mohawk claims would be terminated forever. The State's assertion rested on the dubious land cession agreement made between the United States and Joseph Brant, a Mohawk soldier commissioned during the Revolution as a captain in the British Army. From our perspective the 1797 Brant Treaty was fraudulent since Brant had no authority to sign away our territory, nor was the agreement ever endorsed by the Mohawk Nation Council. Since this was true, we retained clear title to most of our aboriginal territory, for which New York would have to make amends since the State conspired to take it from us.

Our delegation realized our contentions would be tested by the State. Since it was not in a financial position to pay for the theft of our land or the subsequent damages to it, then it would seek to make separate deals with factions within the Mohawk community more susceptible to cash payouts. While this may have worked in the past, we were determined to hold together by pooling our resources and moving the community toward a singular national administration. While negotiating with the United States and the State, we were also drafting a trade and commerce code that would be applied to all of Akwesasne along with a set of civil and criminal laws to be enforced by a joint Mohawk Peacekeeping Service. We needed money to sue the State if the talks failed, so we adopted a strategy of targeting the large corporations that were located on the disputed land and naming them as defendants if we decided to litigate.

The larger claim would be a tremendous task requiring the active participation of all Mohawk communities: Kahnawake, Kanehsatake, Wahta, Tyendinaga, Oshweken, and Akwesasne. This would have meant the expenditure of large financial and physical resources to meet with the residents of each area, provide formal instruction as to the historical basis for the claim, secure consensus, and design a legal strategy to substantiate our historical rights to the 9.9 million acres. It was not simply making an appeal to a collective identity, but for the first time overcoming generations of divisions to forge a common Mohawk front with regards to an issue of paramount importance.

The Mohawks had not acted in unison since hundreds of our ancestors had left the Mohawk Valley homelands 315 years before. But there was reason to hope that if Akwesasne could somehow manage to unify, there was a chance the Mohawk people could march under a single banner with the land claims as its rallying point.

This is what we were planning in 1984. When I spoke about the need to address the 9.9 million acre claim, I knew it would be impossible for the State to concede to our arguments, however persuasive or supported by the law. The State had been born only because it was an active participant in the theft of Iroquois land; it had been weaned on deception, graft, bribery, and lies. It had never acknowledged aboriginal land title and had defied with impunity U.S. federal laws meant to prohibit individual states from taking Indian territory. It could not have existed without the unscrupulous alienation of our lands, nor could it have prospered without denigrating our culture and history. New York State had a single Indian policy throughout its history: deny the viability of the Iroquois as a human being with the right to exist on his own terms. Governor Mario Cuomo's assistants, those men sitting across the negotiating table from us, were not about to change 200 years of sordid history and offer justice to the Mohawk Nation. We knew there would be a hostile reaction to our presentation, but if the State remained a convenient opponent common to all Mohawks, we might be able to secure sufficient concessions which would enable us to expand our land base and grow our economy without having to resort to armed occupations or controversial money-raising schemes such as selling cigarettes or gambling.

After the session in Syracuse we returned to Akwesasne to promote our ideas for unity. Committees were appointed by the three councils to prepare recommendations for ways in which the community would be governed in the near future as a single entity. A Mohawk Nation Justice Code was pre-pared, one that stressed reconciliation, was based on traditional customs, and eliminated the adversarial U.S. courts—New York would have no say in how we handled disputes or meted out punishments. We created a Trade and Commerce Committee to draft one set of laws applicable to all busi-nesses at Akwesasne; the group would also make economic development suggestions to maximize our geographical location astride the St. Lawrence by distributing goods to other Mohawk communities from both Canada and the United States. An inland port was considered, which would have meant ships from other nations could make direct deliveries to Akwesasne; these products would be moved across the continent on our own licensed vehicles.

One of our objectives was to build an economy using the traditional mar-keting skills of the Mohawks. In former times our ancestors played a key role in the delivery of manufactured goods into the continental interior along various waterways. In exchange, the Mohawks carried furs to the markets in the east. The ability to monitor this flow of products to and from markets enabled the Mohawks to secure political influence and achieve material prosperity during the colonial era. Our intent was to replicate this activity by entering into a series of trade compacts with other Native nations. For example, we would deliver oranges and fruits from Seminole territory in Florida to northern Canada and bring back furs, freshwater fish, and craft items made by the woodland Crees to the far south. The end result would have been the reestablishing of an independent Mohawk Nation exercising full, complete, and separate jurisdiction over a part of its ancestral territory, one which was economically prosperous, without having the burdens of an artificial, material-based class structure.

The resolution of the Akwesasne land claims would have provided our joint committee with tens of millions of dollars in revenue to bolster the Mohawk Nation state. We would have secure fiscal independence from U.S. or Canadian government-controlled social programs, which would have been redesigned to conform to our cultural standards. We envisioned a separate education system, an innovative housing plan, universal health care, expanded programs for elders, and guaranteed income for all Mohawk families.

In January 1987 our group issued a formal position paper drafted by St. Regis Tribal Chiefs Rosemary Bonaparte and Brenda Lafrance. All three Mohawk councils endorsed the report. The report emphasized the unity of the claims while summarizing the legal background, which gave us the right to seek redress. It stated that the so-called state treaties which stripped away thousands of acres from Akwesasne were "illegal and void"—that New York State's actions in entering into such agreements, which clearly breached U.S. federal law, had been knowing and deliberate. Our Mohawk negotiating team issued a set of principles and objectives, which stressed our intent to expand our land base, secure compensation for the lost lands, expand our jurisdictional powers, protect our tax-free status, and eliminate the international border at Akwesasne.

A year later, in 1988, we retained the services of appraisers to tell us exactly what we should expect in the way of past damages and current usage fees for the lands in question. The report (which was cited in our settlement proposal of August 16, 1988, as tendered to New York) estimated the value of the lands at over $400 million, from which we could seek over $69 million in annual rental fees. One of our strategies was to target large corporations located on the contested land, then name them as defendants. We would initiate separate discussions with the companies in an effort to secure what one of our attorneys called a financial "war chest" to cover the costs of pending litigation while paying for the proposed economic initiatives.

The collapse of the united Mohawk front began with the arrival of the first mechanical gambling machines in 1986. The traditional Mohawk Nation Council was bound by its own customs, which outlawed gambling, while the Mohawk Council of Akwesasne was bound to adhere to Canadian antigaming statutes. The relaxing of New York State and U.S. federal authority on the American side of the reservation, brought about by the 1979 crisis with its attendant assertion of Native sovereignty, represented an ideal opportunity for individual entrepreneurs to test the economic waters. Gambling had proven to be a success in other Native communities, beginning with the Seminoles of Florida. From there it spread like nasty gossip, with bingo halls and then casinos spreading throughout Indian country.

The ability of the Mohawk Nation Council to control gambling within its ranks was tested in 1986 when a subchief of the Bear Clan was dismissed for conspiring to operate a "bingo jack" gambling hall, but the St. Regis Tribal Council could not apply similar discipline against some of its members. Lacking a police force, there was little the Tribe could do when slot machines were brought to Akwesasne and placed at one of the larger truck stops. Appeals to remove the machines were ignored, and when the Tribe sought the intervention of the state police, its leaders were accused of treason.

The resistance to a united Mohawk community might have begun with the pro-gambling elements but was also of serious concern to the smugglers who had just begun to reap enormous profits from their midnight cigarette runs into Canada, where tobacco taxes were double that of New York State. The smuggling cartel felt they had just cause to oppose a singular Mohawk Nation, which would have sufficient policing powers to affect their operations. In some cases, smuggling profits were used to purchase slot machines, which, as subsequent investigations showed, were obtained from Mafia-run businesses in New Jersey and Nevada. In 1988 the casino-smuggling cartel ran its own candidate in the election for a position as chief on the St. Regis Tribal Council and pulled off a remarkable upset. By three votes out of hundreds cast, the antiunity forces were able to place their man in office. That person, Leo David Jacobs, was determined to put an end to the unification plans. Throughout his six years in office he sought to oust the other two Mohawk councils from the land claims negotiations while pressing for the expansion of casino gambling. The August 1988 land claims settlement proposal represented a high-water mark for the Akwesasne Mohawks in terms of money, land, and jurisdiction. Thereafter, the State negotiators bided their time, knowing the united front was fracturing as the pro-gamblers took effective control over all three Tribal Council positions. By 1990, the dream of one people, one community, and one nation was dead.

In October of 2004 New York Governor George Pataki announced he had reached a land settlement agreement with the three Mohawk councils. A single claim for all of Akwesasne had been revived with the 2003 election to the Tribe of James Ransom, a former employee of the Haudenosaunee Task Force on the Environment, an organization created under the authority of the Mohawk Nation Council. In the spring of 2003 the Tribe had proposed a singular settlement deal that expressly tied the cession of the disputed lands to New York's offer of a casino in the Catskills resort region. The Tribe's electorate soundly defeated this proposal.

The revival of a joint negotiating team from all three Mohawk councils produced a quick alternative that represented an enormous retreat from the 1988 plan. Gone were the challenges to the corporations, the $69 million in rental fees, the demand for exclusive jurisdiction, and the insistence on remaining tax-free. Nothing was stated about securing a clean environment, claiming damages for past degradations, or eliminating the international border. The 2004 deal was valued at $100 million to be paid in annual increments, reduced electrical rates, and the waiver of tuition fees at New York's state universities. The Mohawks had the option of buying up to 13,000 acres of land, but it had to be contiguous to the existing reservation. No broad exemptions from State or U.S. federal authority were sought. Rushed through by the Tribe using a campaign largely based on fear (it is this deal or nothing at all), the package was approved on November 27 by voters on the U.S. and Canadian sides of Akwesasne by very large margins.

But the three clans of the Mohawk Nation, Bear, Wolf, and Turtle, were adamantly opposed to the settlement because they felt it meant the extinguishing for all time of the Mohawk claims to their original lands. In this, Mohawks joined them from other communities who were angered by the lack of consultation during the negotiations. Reassurances by the Nation's negotiators that an exclusion included in the proposal, which would enable the Nation Council to sue at a later date for the 9.9 million acres using aboriginal titles as the bases for such a claim, was met with hostility given that such an argument has never been sustained in the U.S. courts. On December 18, 2004, the Mohawk Nation Council held the second in a series of public meetings to determine what course of action to adopt since it would not be a signatory to the settlement. Tribal and Mohawk Council of Akwesasne officials said they were bound to sign the deal, even if the Nation Council excluded itself. The unity concept was, once again and for at least another generation, ground into dust.

CHAPTER 5

~

Trade and Commerce

Trade and commerce have been essential parts of Iroquois life since long before our arrival in the northeast; their regulation became a critical source of power for the Haudenosaunee, particularly after the arrival of the Europeans in North America. When the Iroquois expanded their communities from the eastern shores of Lake Ontario, they selected areas which were not only rich in natural resources, but strategically positioned along vital inland water routes.

The Mohawks located most of their towns on the shores of the Mohawk and St. Lawrence Rivers in order to monitor trade. The Mohawk River was the easiest way to enter the continental interior from the middle Atlantic coastal region. Products such as seashells, used as articles of adornment, were exchanged for copper bits from the Great Lakes nations. In exchange for permitting trade expeditions to pass through Iroquois territory while using its resources, the Mohawks were able to command payment in goods, while also profiting from providing food, materials, and shelter.

Prior to the arrival of the Europeans, the Native nations had developed an elaborate network of trade routes on and off water. Not only were material goods carried along these highways, but individuals and groups traveled across Iroquois territory as news carriers, messengers, storytellers, and migrants.

The formation of the Haudenosaunee Confederacy enabled the Iroquois to consolidate its commerce powers by stabilizing national borders, reducing warfare, and creating a mutual alliance network through which disputes could be resolved. Periodic grand councils were held at Onondaga, the capital of the Confederacy, to discuss issues of national and international concern.

In the seventeenth century, trade and commerce were central concerns of the Confederacy and had become a life-and-death issue for the Mohawks, in particular. In an era of permanent warfare, whichever nation had access to firearms and gunpowder would be able to dominate their regions. The Mohawks realized the political, military, and economic consequences of controlling access to Europeans' manufactured goods. The flintlock rifle gave them a formidable edge, gradually enabling the Mohawks to eliminate their competitors to the south, east, and north.

Superiority in arms also meant small bands of Mohawks were able to control direct access to the fur markets in Montreal and Albany. The Mohawks would lie in ambush along the Ottawa and St. Lawrence Rivers, waiting for the trappers from the west to bring their pelts to market, only to be hijacked and their cargo taken to Albany. These raids were of considerable concern to the Confederacy since they provoked hostilities among the nations, whose response was to retaliate by declaring war on the Iroquois.

Since France had entered into formal alliances with Native nations in the north, it had no choice but to intervene on behalf of its allies. The Native nations in league with the French did not have the arms or resources to sustain a coordinated invasion of Iroquois territory, but the Europeans did. French armies in the company of Indian fighters struck hard at the Iroquois, only to provoke the Confederacy to launch similar attacks against the Hurons, Crees, and Algonkians, all associated with New France.

In one well-recorded military campaign the Confederacy declared war against the Hurons, a nation which held territory in present-day central Ontario. The Hurons had proven to be the most important Native ally with France and had supplied intelligence and manpower when the French invaded Oneida, Onondaga, and Mohawk territories in the first decades of the 1600s.

The Confederate strategy was to destroy the Huron Nation, absorb its citizens, and strengthen its control over the northern trade routes. In the winter of 1648–1649 the Confederacy kept a large army in the field as it struck a number of Huron towns and nearby Catholic settlements. The thousands of refugees who fled their homes were either absorbed by the Iroquois, found haven in Quebec, or were dispersed among other Native peoples. The Confederacy's elimination of a major trade competitor in the north freed its forces to attack its adversaries in other areas.

The French continued to give aid and support to Iroquois opponents who, despite the loss of some shipments, were able to bypass the Ottawa River route by traveling to the far north. Peace treaties aimed at opening markets were entered into between the Iroquois and France, only to be undermined by the occasional hijacking of furs.

In 1701, terms were reached at a grand assembly held in Montreal, by which a permanent peace accord was reached between the Confederacy and France. The Confederacy had come to realize that the state of perpetual warfare was driving it into physical extinction.

Iroquois trade took another form after 1701. From hijackers to transporters, Iroquois men converted their knowledge of trade routes and river currents into jobs with the Hudson's Bay Company. The Iroquois worked with the French Canadian voyageurs as they made their way west into the prairies and beyond.

By the early decades of the nineteenth century, small bands of Mohawks had elected to settle in the far west. Arriving as traders, the Mohawks brought their families to the Rocky Mountains, where they were welcomed among the Salish, Kootenai, Flathead, and Cree. The Mohawks were hired by the North West Company, a competitor of Hudson's Bay until absorbed by the latter in 1821.

The economies of the Iroquois nations experienced radical changes after the land cessions following the American Revolution. Traditionally, Iroquois women were the primary cultivators of the soil—they planted seeds, weeded fields, and harvested crops. With the restrictions on movement that came from being bound to small land areas, Iroquois men had to adapt to a sedentary lifestyle. Farming for them did not come easy, with the change characterized by widespread alcoholism and domestic violence.

Reform and adjustment came from the teachings of the Seneca prophet Handsome Lake, whose instructions about living in a new way came from a series of visions he experienced in 1799. Handsome Lake told his followers to cultivate their remaining lands while emphasizing the need to abide by the ancestral communal rituals. He was cautious about accepting too many European-based ways while forbidding his adherents from gambling, drinking alcohol, or divorcing their spouses.

Handsome Lake's principles insured the survival of many Iroquois communities whose economies became local. Animals and crops grown using Western technologies enabled many Iroquois farmers to secure a living. Some, particularly the Mohawks, continued to pursue hunting and trapping as a way of life, although in decreasing numbers.

In the early decades of the twentieth century a new outlet for their ancestral skills was found: that of the high steel worker. The Iroquois men discovered an activity that enabled them to secure well-paying jobs and enhanced their reputation as fearless providers eager to travel the old trails, even if they were now covered with asphalt.

In their travels the ironworkers from the northeast met many other Native peoples, some of whom were impressed with the aggressive definition of aboriginal sovereignty that the Iroquois preached both on and off the job. That stance was enhanced when the Iroquois workers successfully defended their right to cross the U.S.–Canadian border in pursuit of their trade using the provisions of the 1794 Jay Treaty as a defense. This was followed by land reclamation initiatives, the founding of the political cultural touring group the White Roots of Peace, and the decidedly pro-Native news publication *Akwesasne Notes* in 1968.

From their divided homeland on the St. Lawrence the Mohawks of Akwesasne urged Native nations to remove the yoke of the Bureau of Indian Affairs and act as sovereign entities in accordance with aboriginal and international law. For some, this represented an opportunity to stimulate economic growth using aboriginal rights to avoid paying state taxes on the sale of goods to non-Natives.

Robert Satiacum, a Native rights fighter from the Pacific Northwest, heeded the Mohawk message. In 1977 he used his status as a Puyallup heredity chief to open the first tax-free Indian tobacco stand along with a small casino, the first among any Native nation.

Forced by the United States to close his operations in 1978, Satiacum was convicted on racketeering, contraband tobacco trafficking, gambling, and arson charges. He fled the United States to Canada, where he was given political refugee status, only to be arrested for sexual assault on a minor in British Columbia. Satiacum died in jail on March 25, 1991, while awaiting trial.

Despite his failings, Satiacum's business ventures were noted across the country, with other Native entrepreneurs cautiously following suit. From small, roadside cigarette stands to commercial bingo halls, Native nations were in a position to profit from the political and legal victories of the Indian rights movement.

The Seminoles of Florida, followed by the Oneidas of New York, gingerly tested the legal waters when they opened large bingo halls. When other nations saw the states lose their legal challenges to regulate bingo gambling in U.S. federal courts, they opened their own halls. Within a few short years, large steel butler buildings, smoky, unadorned, with the interiors dominated by massive screens lighting up numbers from 1 to 75, could be found on the main roads of reservations from Maine to California.

The issue confronting the Iroquois was whether this form of economic development could be sustained given the specific prohibitions against gambling contained in the Handsome Lake Code, that series of rules which saved most of them from cultural extinction. At Onondaga, the capital of the Haudenosaunee Confederacy, the position of the governing council was unambiguous: no gambling, regardless of its potential benefits or subtle disguise. In Oneida, at Akwesasne and Kahnawake, and among the Senecas of Cattaraugus Allegheny, warnings about the perils of commercial gambling were pushed aside in favor of an activity that created badly needed jobs and a source of income outside of the miniscule federal, state, and provincial aide, which came with a web of sticky strings.

In the spring of 1984 the new economy was brought to Akwesasne in a plain black Chevrolet van driven by Philip Deering, a resident of the Mohawk community of Kahnawake. As the editor of the community newspaper, I was intrigued by Mr. Deering's position that Akwesasne's unique geographical location could actually be of tangible benefit in the marketing of tobacco products. Mr. Deering was accompanied by Thomas Delaronde, one of the leaders of the Ganienkeh community recently established on the northern edge of the Adirondacks west of Plattsburgh. The residents there were looking for a way to make an income, with bingo and tobacco having great appeal.

My concern was the lack of control by the Mohawk Nation Council over activities which, if as profitable as Deering and Delaronde suggested, might well undermine the Nation's authority if individuals acted on their own initiative, using the collective rights of the Mohawks as a shield.

Deering and Delaronde were well aware of the hard-fought battles at Akwesasne to secure greater independence from external agencies. They had taken part in a series of intense discussions as part of a group called the Iroquois Land Rights Committee, which conducted public hearings in many communities to define aboriginal sovereignty and how to prosper under its umbrella. The members of the land rights group were convinced there was an alternative to the seasonal jobs, crafts work, and public assistance programs which then constituted the main income for many Iroquois families. Environmental degradation, soil exhaustion, and a rapid growth in population meant a decrease in the number of farms, while the heavily polluted waters flowing through most Iroquois reservations had caused the fishing and trapping occupations to collapse.

Deering and Delaronde believed there was a real opportunity to make money which would then underwrite existing community programs as well as provide resources for expansion into other areas, including gambling. I knew both men—they were resourceful, experienced, and determined to do what they thought was right for the Mohawk people. But securing the approval of the Mohawk Nation Council would take time, and there were personal, communal, and international implications which needed careful study. The men were visiting our offices to see if we would endorse the tobacco trade prior to a formal presentation to the Council.

On March 14, 1985, almost a year after the Deering-Delaronde visit, the Iroquois Land Rights Committee submitted its findings to the Grand Council of the Haudenosaunee. The committee itself was composed of members from all Six Nations. Among its recommendations were

- the establishment of a Haudenosaunee Trade and Commerce Commission to assist the Grand Council in the regulating of economic development;
- the development of a set of rules governing tobacco sales, the marketing of petroleum products, and gambling operations;
- the formation of a political action committee to counter New York State or U.S. federal policies that might affect economic development plans;
- the determination of the merits of nationalizing certain businesses on Iroquois territory.

The land rights group was clear on another point: "The only sure route to controlling the economic development issue before us seems to be by way of nationalizing control over those developments that hold the potential for creating very wealthy individuals and power cliques within our communities."

While the Trade and Commerce Commission was, in fact, established by the Haudenosaunee, its actual administrative authority was challenged, then fatally undermined by some of the Land Rights group, who had, by that time, already become immersed in either the gambling or tobacco businesses. They were not about to subject the sources of this newfound wealth to any external government, including their own.

In the spring of 1986 the Mohawk Nation Council of Chiefs authorized the creation of a special committee to draft policies aimed at regulating tobacco and petroleum sales at Akwesasne. The committee, of which I was a member, worked in conjunction with the St. Regis Tribal Council and the Mohawk Council of Akwesasne since regulatory uniformity was the only way to control both activities, which had come to dominate the economic lives of the Mohawks. Our proposed rules were enacted by the Mohawk Nation in May of that year but were openly defied by many of the tobacco and motor fuel retailers. Without an effective enforcement arm the laws were ignored.

For many Mohawks the smuggling of low-cost cigarettes from the United States into Canada, where they were subject to high federal and provincial taxes, represented an opportunity to make a lot of money with minimal risk. During the Prohibition era the St. Lawrence River region, including Akwesasne, had become a smuggler's dream. Alcohol of all kinds was carried by boat from Ontario or Quebec, then driven in modified vehicles to outlets in New England and New York City. Two generations later, those same routes were being used to carry hundreds of thousands of cases of cigarettes north into Canada for resale in Montreal, Ottawa, and Toronto.

Alliances were made with Chinese tongs and Vietnamese street gangs to distribute the cigarettes; they, in return, paid thousands of dollars to the Mohawks to smuggle illegal aliens from Asia into the United States. Later, the Hell's Angels would show up on the reservation looking to buy cheap assault weapons and explosives to use against their opponents in the Ontario and Quebec drug trade.

Some of the profits from smuggling went toward underwriting the construction of the casinos at Akwesasne followed by offshore banking, purchases of Florida real estate, and the building of massive private homes on both sides of the border.

The anarchy at Akwesasne was repeated in other Iroquois communities. At Tuscarora, near Niagara Falls, New York, one business owner openly boasted about becoming the first Native billionaire, and on other reservations the tobacco and fuel station owners had taken over the reigns of power, using intimidation, bribery, and outright acts of terror against their opponents.

In 1995 the gambling controversy exploded at Cattaraugus, where three people were killed after a shootout, while at Onondaga, two business owners were banished for life for their defiance of that nation's laws. Among the Oneidas, the situation was also tense when community members asked for an accounting of the Turning Stone casino revenues while supporting the Confederacy's decision to remove the so-called nation representative in 1993. Because of these actions, dozens of Oneidas were stripped of all their benefits and their homes were subjected to demolition, followed by a decision to ban them from all properties owned by the Oneida Nation.

The Haudenosaunee Confederacy did not stand idly by while the nations descended into chaos. In August 1996 a delegation from each of the Six Nations was selected to meet with New York State officials to discuss how to control tobacco sales on Indian territory. The first session was held in a small conference room in the state capitol. Nine and a half years before, on January 20, 1987, the State's Department of Taxation and Finance had issued a draft set of regulations to assess taxes on reservation tobacco sales to non-Natives.

The Mohawk Nation responded with a counterproposal dated November 30, 1988, in which all three Mohawk councils would assess their own charges on all tobacco sales to be used to underwrite community programs. On March 7, 1990, the Seneca Nation of Cattaraugus-Allegheny (distinct from the Seneca Nation of Tonwanada), a non-Confederate entity created in 1848, entered into a tax revenue–sharing agreement with New York, only to have the Native retailers react by accusing its leadership of fatally compromising Iroquois sovereignty. So intense was the criticism, with a strong possibility of physical harm being brought against the Seneca leaders, that the deal was scuttled almost as soon as it was revealed.

The leadership knew, however, that they needed to secure New York's participation in halting all tobacco deliveries to the reservation, exempting only those with a specific license from the Mohawks. New York would not agree to this, so once again, the three Mohawk councils had no means to stop deliveries short of confiscating the wholesalers' trucks. This was tried, once, in December 1986, when a transport vehicle with a quarter million dollars' worth of cigarettes was impounded by the Nation. The reaction of the retailers was immediate. They created a group called the Six Nations Warrior Society to counter any attempt to stop deliveries. Faced with inevitable confrontation, the three councils retreated from enforcing the tobacco codes.

The need to forge a trade agreement with New York State was obvious to the Haudenosaunee. The freewheeling tobacco trade had made millionaires of many Iroquois, while the vast majority lived at or beneath economic poverty levels. The nations needed a source of revenue to deliver basic services and to wean the Iroquois off state and federal aid. By controlling the importation and distribution of tobacco products to the retailers, the Confederacy would realize an immediate source of income, while removing the source of power by the tobacco cartels. The challenge was to convince the State that such a plan was in its own interests.

The Haudenosaunee began the August 19, 1996, meeting by reciting the Ohenten Kariwatekwen. Since the prayer was in Iroquois, the State's delegates did not understand its content, but they could see how it placed the Iroquois in an agreeable state of mind. The State's position appeared to be strong. It had favorable court decisions which it could enforce on the wholesalers prior to making reservation deliveries. The Iroquois, on the other hand, were splintered, with no apparent means to compel the retailers to abide by the Confederacy's decisions.

The State was insistent its taxes must be collected on sales to non-Natives and remanded to Albany on tobacco and fuel. It wanted all vendors to be registered with Albany, the right to control wholesalers making deliveries to the reservations, the right to prohibit out-of-state fuel deliveries to Native gas stations, the right to require Natives to sign tax exemption forms at the time of purchase, and the authority to compel the Iroquois to set retail prices at or close to those of their non-Native competitors.

The Haudenosaunee did not respond with anger or alarm. They knew there would be no concessions on sovereignty issues and that no taxes would be paid to New York. They would not permit State officials to license Native retailers or allow troopers on Indian land to enforce any provisions of the State's tax code. The Iroquois delegates knew it would take some time to arrive at a compact that strengthened rather than qualified their status as independent peoples. They also realized the need to conduct further negotiations with an eye toward security since disruptions by the retailers were certain, as would be the accusations of treason.

The August meeting went well, although the Iroquois were not about to put aside generations of mistrust by believing the State would actually dull the sharpness of its fangs. But one historical event marked the August session: it was the first time New York State acknowledged there was such a thing as a Grand Council of the Haudenosaunee Confederacy.

Over the course of the fall, winter, and spring of 1996–1997 the Haudenosaunee held many meetings with New York officials on the proposed trade and commerce compact. As the months passed, the New York negotiators began to slowly move toward the Iroquois perspective on trade and taxes. Onondaga Nation leaders Chief Irving Powless and Faithkeeper Oren Lyons demonstrated their abilities as diplomats by keeping the discussions creative, even as tensions were rising. The retailers knew the meetings were taking place and had begun a campaign to undermine the Confederacy's plans. They were of the opinion that no government, Native or not, was going to monitor their actions or affect their profits. The State's negotiating team was warned repeatedly by the Haudensoaunee about the confrontational tactics the retailers would use once a deal was reached. The State was told such events would be tailored to the media and magnified beyond reality by individuals who knew how to manipulate the press.

The talks moved ahead. The Haudenosaunee did not waiver from their original position—no state taxes, Haudenosaunee-issued permits, no state examination of the businesses licensed by the Haudenosaunee, no IDs to be shown to the retailers, no enforcement of U.S. court decisions on Iroquois territory, and no interference with Native nation-to-nation trade. The Haudenosaunee would create a singular wholesale outlet at Onondaga, which would be the only way for retailers to order tobacco products. The Haudenosaunee also insisted that the 1794 Canandaigua Treaty be respected, particularly its provisions respecting Iroquois jurisdiction over its own lands.

Gradually, the outline of a trade compact took real form. The State realized the problem was not with the Haudenosaunee, but with the economic anarchy that the retailers had brought about in defiance of their own national councils. By working with the Haudenosaunee, order could be restored and the bulk of the tobacco sales revenues directed toward real government services defined and administered by the Iroquois themselves. A stronger, more stable and prosperous Haudenosaunee made good business and political sense, while reducing State expenditures on policing, social services, and governmental operations across the board.

By April 1997, a final compact was ready to be submitted to Governor Pataki and to the Grand Council of the Haudenosaunee. But while the Iroquois delegates accurately predicted a wave of orchestrated protests, they did not expect the entire deal to be scuttled by Pataki because of the intense anticompact lobbying activities of the Oneida Nation of New York. Since the Oneida Nation was declared outlaw by the Grand Council in May 1993, it had become apprehensive about the Haudenosaunee growing in strength and possibly affecting its lucrative gambling operations. Powerful politicians were swayed by the Oneidas to call upon Pataki to refrain from signing the compact. At the same time, interstate highways 90 and 81, both of which pass through Iroquois territory, were blocked by small groups of Iroquois subjected to the wild distortions about the agreement by the retailers and their "warrior" allies. The road blockages in May 1997 provided Pataki with the rationale he needed to refute the trade and commerce compact.

The Haudenosaunee leadership was taken by surprise. They knew the protests were shallow and could not be sustained beyond a few days. They had good reason to expect the Iroquois people would, once the terms of the agreement were released, endorse the compact. They were prepared to carry it on even after the home of Tuscarora Chief Leo Henry was destroyed by fire while others on the Iroquois negotiating team faced similar dangers. If they could withstand the pressure, they had no reason to believe Pataki would concede as quickly as he did.

The 1997 Trade and Commerce Agreement, had it been approved, would have revolutionized State–Iroquois relations if for no other reason than it would have marked the first time New York would be bound to deal with the Haudenosaunee as a governing entity with the exclusive authority to regulate commerce on territories upon which the Confederacy exercised active jurisdiction. The deal was defeated, and Haudenosaunee–State relations reverted to apprehension and mistrust.

CHAPTER 6

The Cayuga Decisions: A Call to Action

When I was a teenager in the late 1960s and early 1970s, it was a unique time to be a young Akwesasne Mohawk. By 2004, all young Iroquois were experiencing quite different realities in a world defined by cynicism, avarice, factionalism, and dismay.

Our community a generation past was a beehive of political, social, and cultural activities; the traditional people were on the move, with the Mohawk Nation Council overseeing the publication of the godfather of all Native news journals, *Akwesasne Notes,* sponsoring the touring group White Roots of Peace, holding conferences to discuss aboriginal rights, and being an overall pain in the rear to the Bureau of Indian Affairs and other right-wing organizations.

The ancient ceremonies which define our relationship with the universe, labeled "pagan rituals" by some, attracted great support among the younger generation and fitted well with the social activism of that era. Our dances and songs excited our emotions while liberating us from the shackles of Christian shame. We felt good about who we were, and that alone was a threat to many.

Our community was a magnet for Native peoples from throughout the world. At the offices of *Akwesasne Notes,* where we went to help mail the newspaper, one could at any time meet Aborigines from Australia, Lakotas from Pine Ridge, Mapuchis from Chile, or Mayans from the hills of Guatemala, the grandparents of all Turtle Island indigenous people.

We not only learned from our visitors, but they took with them a distinctly Haudenosaunee perspective on this thing called Native identity. They were taught to be firm in their defense of the natural world, to aggressively pursue their treaty rights, and to never concede anything to the external judicial or political entities who had no desire to see an expansion of our aboriginal nations. These judges and congressmen were agents of a system that barely tolerated our survival as distinct peoples.

Courts and lawyers, presidents and senators, and bills and appeals had no place in our councils because our traditional leaders adhered to a different set of values. They took to heart their responsibilities to speak on behalf of the natural world and those yet unborn. They were, in the Western capitalistic sense, truly impractical leaders, but their determination to remain true to the ancestral ways ignited fires throughout the hemisphere.

As a teenager, the longhouse people won my support because they took a strong stand against the system. The Mohawk Nation had good reason to stand tall as its citizens put their bodies on the line in defense of their Native rights. Mohawks blocked bridges, occupied offices, and reclaimed land. Our citizens led the takeover of Alcatraz, played a key role in the 1972 Bureau of Indian Affairs takeover, and joined with the Lakota Nation at Wounded Knee.

Along the way, we mastered the art of mass communication beginning with our own publications, which not only offered a pro-Native newspaper, but printed books and posters which could be found on the shelves and hanging on the walls of Native homes and offices across America. An Akwesasne Mohawk was greeted with warmth and admiration for we were seen as a people who refused to knuckle under.

The events I witnessed were all the more amazing given the composition of the Mohawk Nation Council of Chiefs. The *rotiiane* (our traditional male leaders), clanmothers, and faithkeepers were not highly educated in the formal sense. They were basket weavers, ironworkers, fishermen, and lacrosse stick makers. They thought and conversed almost entirely in the Mohawk language and held conservative views on the sanctity of marriage, the care of children, and the need to preserve a sharp distinction between the genders.

The Nation Council met in the old longhouse every Sunday. Their meetings were dignified affairs, characterized by long silences, gentle questions, and respectful discussions—one never heard a harsh word or a loud, argumentative voice. The passions of the day were often carried into the longhouse by the younger crowd, but after the recitation of the Onhenton Karihwatekwen, the words of thanksgiving which must come before all else. Those words, as spoken by one of the *rotiiane* holding a string of sacred wampum, addressed the natural world and gave us a sense of perspective as to who we were as Onkwehonwe, Kaiienkehaka, and Haudenosaunee.

The prayer also affirmed our place within creation as well as acknowledged our connection with the spiritual world. We realized the earth was a living entity and very conscious of the humans who walked on her. We saw ourselves as defenders of the natural world whenever we rallied to oppose unwarranted intrusions into our community by Canada or the United States. Given this powerful sense of belonging, how could we lose?

One of the goals of the Mohawk Nation was to secure additional lands as Akwesasne had become a fairly crowded place with a dramatic population increase after World War II. The longhouse people were also concerned about the contamination of our water, air, and land from a number of industrial plants on our western borders. Along with the other Iroquois nations, the Mohawks initiated a formal land claim against New York because we believed the State had violated our treaties as well as U.S. federal law when it allegedly purchased Mohawk territory. The Mohawks watched as the Oneidas and Cayugas won a series of legal victories in the U.S. courts which should have ideally stimulated serious settlement negotiations. But there were those traditional Mohawks who were apprehensive about taking our land claims into court. They saw how the Iroquois were defeated when they sought justice in the 1950s. The struggles to prevent the construction of Kinzua Dam on Seneca territory; the building of a huge water reservoir on the Tuscarora reservation; the ripping apart of parts of Akwesasne and Kahnawake to build the St. Lawrence Seaway—in each instance the Iroquois had taken their complaints into state and federal courts, only to lose. Naturally, there was considerable apprehension by the chiefs and clanmothers. They knew the courts were controlled by non-Native white males who had limited understanding of Iroquois issues and no tolerance for the Haudenosaunee's insistence on maintaining its independence from the United States.

Land occupations were effective, but there was a high risk of confrontation and violence, as shown in the Eagle Bay encampment of 1974. New Yorkers were, on the whole, opposed to any attempt by the Haudenosaunee to exercise their status as nations. When the Cayugas were closing in on a $6 million settlement deal in 1979, the residents of the claim area organized an effective campaign to sabotage it, which only served to confirm the fears of the other nations.

Despite these setbacks, the Oneidas residing in New York pressed their claims and overcame the odds by winning their case before the U.S. Supreme Court. That decision affirmed that New York was in breach of U.S. federal law when it entered into "treaties" with ethnic Iroquois without the approval of Congress.

Surely, some believed, that would have compelled New York to come to the bargaining table with a serious commitment to resolve the land claims issue. Instead, the State elected to delay any serious discussions while it designed strategies to undermine any effort by the Haudenosaunee to present a united front.

Commercial gambling in the way of casino options in exchange for a limited claims settlement was dangled in front of the Iroquois by former New York Governor Mario Cuomo, then was later adopted by his successor, George Pataki. Gambling was offensive to traditional Iroquois, but state officials were aware of the divisions within each Native community. By dealing with the weakest cultural faction, New York expected to get out of its land claims dilemma cheaply.

The first break occurred among the Akwesasne Mohawks. Split into three factions as the result of the imposition of colonial tribal and band councils, both of which were designed to undermine the traditional Mohawk Nation Council, the Mohawks were hard pressed to sustain internal unity. In 1985 the St. Regis Tribal Council faction sanctioned a commercial bingo operation; the next year, slot machines were brought in from Las Vegas over which there were no controls.

The rise in illicit gambling was paced with tobacco and alcohol smuggling into Canada, activities the Nation Council did not have the resources to stop. The Mohawks were not the only ones moving into gambling as the cornerstone of economic development. The Oneidas and Senecas opened bingo halls, with the Oneida operation subject to accusations of mismanagement and graft.

All of these actions factored into the Cayuga land claims. Whenever the Iroquois had acted in unity, as demonstrated throughout the 1970s, New York retreated. Now that the Iroquois were in-fighting, the State felt no pressure to resolve any of the claims.

In December 1998 the Oneida Nation of New York set off an anti-Native firestorm when it decided to include 20,000 homeowners as defendants in its land claim. Previous to that action, there was a small group called the Upstate Citizens for Equality (UCE), formed to oppose the Oneida Nation's gambling, gas, and tobacco businesses. They were vocal, but marginal. The December decision gave UCE an ideal opportunity to enlist thousands of homeowners and small business operators and thereby command the attention of regional politicians as well as the media. Pressure was being brought to bear on the State to resist any compromises with the Iroquois on any issue, including land.

A chapter of the UCE was formed in the Cayuga homeland region expressly to deny the Cayugas reservation status were they to obtain land within the

64,000 acres they lost as a result of New York's disputed "treaties" of 1795 and 1807. Since that time, the Cayugas have lived on the Cattaraugus Seneca reservation south of Buffalo, New York, on the Grand River Reserve west of Hamilton, Ontario, or as part of the Seneca-Cayuga Tribe of northeastern Oklahoma.

As the trial date approached, U.S. District Court Judge Neal McCurn made a number of rulings which were disturbing to the Iroquois. McCurn excluded land as compensation for the Cayuga losses. If they received anything, it would be money. McCurn then decided the Cayugas would not be allowed to testify as to their cultural losses and physical injuries, stating the plaintiffs must restrict their testimony to a real estate appraisal as to the current value of the original reservation.

Previous to this, McCurn had encouraged negotiations as a way of securing a settlement. To effect that, an arbitrator had been agreed on to bring the different parties together. Joining the Cayuga side were officials from the U.S. Justice Department, an act which enraged groups such as UCE. Believing the negotiations would bear fruit if removed from public scrutiny, a gag order was imposed on the Cayugas and State officials, effectively preventing them from communicating to their respective constituents.

This failure to address the more extreme charges brought by UCE against the Cayugas placed the Native negotiators at a great disadvantage. They could not respond to accusations by their opponents that the Cayuga Nation intended to open a casino or would soon sponsor gas stations and smoke shops on whatever land they got back.

The Akwesasne experience taught the Mohawks that public support, both Native and non-Native, was essential if any land deal was to pass through the State Legislature before being passed on to Congress for ratification. Prior to the disintegration of Akwesasne unity in 1989, the Mohawk had drafted a plan for negotiations which included an aggressive public relations campaign that could have resolved many of the fears the non-Natives had about an expansion of Iroquois jurisdiction. Also, the Mohawks presented the State with a comprehensive list of its land claim objectives, all of which were directed at restoring their aboriginal relationship with the earth.

The Cayugas were prevented from doing any of these things, which weakened their bargaining position considerably. Over 200 years of anguish were reduced to dry numbers numbingly recited by real estate appraisers who knew nothing about the Cayuga struggles to remain a people.

The Cayugas' lawyers also lacked the fighting spirit which might have made a difference in the trial. They did not understand the deep feelings the

Cayugas have for their homeland which prevented them from accepting New York's offer of $130 million if only they would agree to restrict their land purchases to 10,000 acres (plus another 3,000 acres of a "forever wild" section), abandon all aboriginal claims, and abide by a future trade and commerce compact. Missing were any references to the treaties of Canandaigua or Ft. Stanwix; gone was the power of the words as spoken by the Haudenosaunee in defense of their homelands.

The Cayugas demonstrated the traditional Haudenosaunee impracticality by turning down the State's final offer. U.S. officials also wanted the Cayugas to take the money since the federal government's offer to pay half the settlement amount was temporary. Still, the Cayugas would not sell.

The trial began in late January 2000 in Syracuse, New York, a city which itself sits in the middle of a land claim set to be filed by the Onondaga Nation. A change of venue motion by the Cayuga lawyers was denied. Nine jurors were selected, some of whom lived in the Onondaga claim area. The Cayuga lawyers did not call on any historian who might have enlightened the jury as to the situation of their clients but instead elected to follow New York's strategy of relying on the appraisers. Their expert fixed the value of the Cayuga reservation at $335.1 million, in contrast to the New York State appraiser, who testified the land was worth only $51 million. After two weeks of listening to those figures the jury retired to make its decision.

On February 17, 2000, the jury tendered its verdict. The Cayugas would receive $35 million based on a price of $576 per acre at current value. They would also get $1.9 million for rental fees over the past 204 years. The Cayuga lawyer referred to the decision as "irrational" and promised an immediate appeal, an action which could very well take several years before a final decision is reached.

Absent from the Cayuga case were the rallies and demonstrations, the pickets and songs which marked Iroquois struggles of the recent past. Exhausted by years of in-fighting, there was little enthusiasm among the Iroquois for taking to the streets or to occupy land which rightfully belongs to the Cayuga Nation. New York was not held liable for the $36.9 million—it could conceivably move to collect that sum from the residents within the claim area, which in turn would make it much more difficult for the Cayugas to return home.

The words of caution from the Iroquois elders about entering a "white man's court," that justice could not be secured in a system which had for so long been used to destroy the Iroquois, were once again affirmed.

By the fall of 2004, the Cayuga case had taken another form. The Seneca-Cayuga Tribe of Oklahoma had been making small ventures into their ancient homelands in an attempt to lend credence to their argument that they, as direct descendants of the Cayuga Nation, had a valid right to be included in any and all land settlement negotiations.

The northeastern Oklahoma group settled in that area after a long journey from New York State which began in the mid-1700s. Small groups of Iroquois had moved into the Ohio region, where they established communities composed of several nations, including the Wyandots (Hurons) from central Ontario. One of the larger groups, primarily Seneca, elected to dwell on the southern shores of Lake Erie in what is now Sandusky, Ohio. They were joined by the Cayugas prior to, and after, the War of 1812.

Two reservations were set aside for the Seneca-Cayugas in 1819, which also included Shawnees, Mohawks, Oneidas, and Onondagas. These two land areas were ceded in 1831 at the insistence of President Andrew Jackson, who vigorously pursued the removal of all Native people west of the Mississippi. The Iroquois bands suffered the death of hundreds of their people on the march west. They arrived in northeastern Oklahoma in 1832 to live on what was called the Neosho reservation.

Far from being alienated from their Iroquois kin in the east, the Oklahoma group continued to travel back and forth, while offering reservation land to anyone wishing to move to Neosho. The reservation was carved up into individual allotments as a result of the 1887 Dawes Act, with over 10,000 acres of excess property sold to non-Natives.

While the annuity payments for the Ohio reservation were terminated in the 1880s, the Seneca-Cayugas continued to receive funds from New York State based on the sale of the Cayuga reservation on the north shore of Cayuga Lake. The Cayuga group in New York has vehemently denied the Oklahoma claims, adopting the State's position that no Native group outside of state boundaries could submit a land claim.

The Seneca-Cayugas made attempts to secure recognition from the Haudenosaunee as a whole in 2003 but were rebuffed, as was its offer to create a trade and commerce compact between them and the New York State–based nations. Any hopes of a united front by the Cayugas from Oklahoma, New York, and Ontario were dashed, which greatly enhanced the negotiating powers of New York State.

In a reversal that stunned the New York Iroquois, Governor George Pataki announced in November 2004 that he would enter into a land claims settlement deal with the Seneca-Cayugas. In exchange for a gambling compact enabling the Oklahoma band to operate a casino in the lucrative Catskills region, they agreed to pay state taxes on all goods sold to non-Natives, remit to Albany funds to cover any and all costs for other Cayuga deals, and to abandon for all time their territorial claims in New York State.

The settlement clearly stimulated the New York Cayugas to reach their own deal. On November 18, 2004, barely one week after the Oklahoma agreement, they announced the securing of a claims resolution which included the right to operate their own Catskills casino, a price parity provision in which products sold to non-Natives would be close to existing state tax rates, a withdrawal of its legal action for $1.7 billion in damages, a rejection of any eviction action against non-Natives from the claim area, the acceptance of $150 million from the Seneca-Cayugas in lieu of State payments for lost lands, a restriction confining them to a 2,500-acre reservation near Cayuga Lake, and the payment, by the Cayugas, of $3 million per year for the duration of the gambling compact to the local counties in New York for any lost revenues caused by the creation of the reservation.

For the Haudenosaunee the Cayuga experience is an example of the perils of factionalism. Despite their firm stances on taxation, jurisdiction, land tenure, and treaties, none of these were sufficient to deter the Cayuga groups from pursuing their own interests with little or no regard as to the effects on the Iroquois as a whole.

CHAPTER 7

Oneida

My first experience with the contemporary Oneida took place at a Grand Council of the Haudenosaunee Confederacy in 1986. As editor of a weekly newspaper serving the Akwesasne community and the bimonthly international news journal *Akwesasne Notes,* my task was to provide readers with information about events in Iroquois territory. I had also been asked to serve as a negotiator on the land claims committee for the Mohawk Nation and as a result, I attended many Grand Council sessions at our capital of Onondaga.

The proceedings of the Council adhered to the strict procedures set by the founders of the Haudenosaunee Confederacy in the distant past. The Council consisted of the Six Nations within the Confederacy itself, each one of which decided whom to send as a formal delegate to the Onondaga sessions.

A Grand Council could be called into assembly by any of the member nations by sending a string of wampum by personal messenger. A summation of the reasons for the meeting was delivered to the nations by the messenger, or runner, along with the time when the Council would meet. Once the nations accepted the wampum, they were obligated to attend the session, where they returned the stringed, tubular beads to the Onondaga Nation.

Each Council begins with the reciting of the Ohenton Karihwatekwen. During the Council the delegates are seated according to their nation. The Mohawks and Senecas are considered the "older bothers" or "uncles" of the Confederacy and sit as one group on the north side of the Onondaga longhouse. They form a kind of upper house throughout the deliberations. The Cayugas, Oneidas, and Tuscaroras sit across from the older brothers on the south side of the building—they are the "younger brothers" or "nephews." The Onondagas sit along the eastern wall of the structure, serving both as hosts and arbitrators during the discussions.

All motions to be considered by the Grand Council are introduced to the floor by the Mohawks. The subject of debate is then discussed by the lower house, the nephews, who need to arrive at a consensus on the issue before taking it across the central fire to the uncles. The debate will go back and forth, with the Onondagas intervening to clarify details. Once the uncles have reached an agreement, the issue is given to the Onondagas for final approval, remanded back for further debate, or vetoed by being placed aside, pending action at a later time.

No person, other than the official delegates, may address the Council unless specifically asked to speak by the Onondagas and with the approval of the other nations. Among the Onondagas sits the leader, Tadodaho, who serves as chairman of the Grand Council, insuring the meeting adheres to custom and the issues are given full consideration prior to action.

I had attended many Grand Councils beginning in 1977 when the Confederacy met to prepare for a presentation to be given on indigenous rights at the United Nations' nongovernmental organization conference in Geneva, Switzerland. From that time to 1986 I had heard of the intense struggles taking place among the Oneidas with regard to their efforts to regain parts of their aboriginal homelands in central New York State, most of which were lost soon after the American Revolution.

I thought it was ironic that the Oneidas were the first Native nation to be dispossessed of their land and driven westward given the loyalty some of them had shown toward the Americans during the Revolution. Despite the most solemn assurances of the United States, an entity which might not have existed had it not been for the Oneidas, they were the ones who suffered the greatest indignities at the hands of their allies.

I believed the fateful decision by some Oneidas to break with the Confederacy and fight on the side of the Americans was a shameful act since it caused a civil war among the Haudenosaunee and came very close to destroying the Confederacy. Yet, 200 years later, the decendents of the pro-American Oneidas were once again sitting at the Grand Council, while at the same time making public pronouncements about their past service to the United States, as if this was somehow a source of pride for the Oneidas and required the Americans to give them special privileges and recognition.

For the Haudenosaunee, the Oneida actions during the 1770s continued to plague the Iroquois since it shattered our united front and led directly to the loss of our ancestral lands. I thought an apology was in order, not a reminder of one of the most shameful acts in our history.

Very few Oneidas remained in central New York after 1840, when they had either relocated to Wisconsin or found refuge in western Ontario. The Marble Hill faction, a Christian group living south of the city of Sherrill, New York, was the only collective remnant of the Oneidas to remain in their homeland territory. A few Oneida families lived at Onondaga, while others lingered on near a small plot of land south of Oneida, New York. By the twentieth century, Oneida territory had been reduced from its 3.5 million acres to an eroded, infertile 32 located on the eastern slope of Peterborough Hill, which cast a long shadow over the miniscule territory.

Each of the six Haudenosaunee nations has, as a token of its legitimacy, a span of wampum referred to as its "council fire." If a nation can no longer fulfill its obligations under the Great Law of the Confederacy, its council fire is held in trust at Onondaga, the wampum keepers of the Haudenosaunee, until such a time as it is once again able to assume its rightful place as a national government.

This had occurred with the Mohawks, who were forced to flee from their capital towns in the Mohawk Valley during the Revolution. Almost all of the Mohawks moved to Canada, although there were occasional efforts to return to their ancestral homes, a dream New York State most emphatically opposed. The Mohawks did, however, take their traditional forms of administration with them, although the council fire remained at Onondaga.

In 1882 the Mohawks of Akwesasne applied at Onondaga for the council fire to be given to them and for the seat of the Mohawk Nation to be located on their territory astride the St. Lawrence River. This was agreed to, and from that time Akwesasne has been the seat of the Mohawk Nation Council.

The Oneidas were in a similarly precarious position in the early 1800s. They were subject to so many internal tensions and factions they could not sustain a national governing agency. The council fire wampum for the Oneidas was given to the Onondaga Nation in expectation that one day, there would be an official Oneida Nation Council composed of the requisite number of chiefs, clanmothers, and faithkeepers capable of administering to the needs of all Oneidas and that such a council would be located somewhere upon their ancestral territory.

This had not taken place by 1986, so there was no Oneida Nation Council with the appropriate council fire. The Wisconsin Oneidas were governed by a "business committee" that adhered to the dictates of the Bureau of Indian Affairs, while the Oneidas of the Thames (also called the Southwold Oneidas) in western Ontario had a band council system as defined by, and responsive to, the Canadian Indian Act.

There was a traditional council for the Oneidas in Southwold. This group was the only Oneida one that reflected the traditional customs and procedures of the Great Law and could make a strong argument that it had existed from time immemorial and was therefore most capable of assuming the council fire wampum. The one issue was the location of the traditional council. If provisions could be made to relocate its chiefs and clanmothers back to the homelands, then the council fire could be rekindled and the Oneidas returned to their rightful place within the circle of the Confederacy.

Such was the dream, and intent, of the most politically active Oneidas, from their dispersal to the 1980s. When the Oneidas were at their lowest ebb in the 1920s, the sisters Mary Cornelius Winder and Delia Cornelius Waterman began a decades-long campaign to establish a homeland within the traditional boundaries of the Oneida Nation, a place where all Oneidas could return and where they would select their leaders in accordance with traditional law. The sisters wrote letters to U.S. officials, pleading their case, but were ignored. They held innumerable meetings among the Oneida and even formed a provisional government, with Mary Winder as president, to press for a redress of their land claims.

Mary Winder died in 1954, but others built on her efforts. An Oneida Council was empowered by the Oneida people to initiate a lawsuit against New York State for its deliberate violation of the 1790 Federal Non-intercourse Act, a law passed by Congress and signed by George Washington at the specific request of the Iroquois, whose leaders rightfully feared that the State's lust for Indian lands would soon leave the Native people with no territory at all.

The lawsuit began to wind its way through the courts in 1970 and was marked by a series of unfavorable decisions, which the Oneidas challenged at every step. They won a major victory in 1974 when the U.S. Supreme Court sustained the Oneida argument that the Non-intercourse Act did in fact apply to the 13 original colonies, while stating that Native lands could not be ceded without U.S. federal approval.

Despite growing animosity among the various groups that claimed to represent all Oneidas, they once again returned to the U.S. Supreme Court, where, in 1985, they scored another win. This time, the Court held that local counties were liable for damages arising out of the illegal taking of Oneida land.

Still, the Court's rulings did nothing to heal the internal divisions that were undermining the ultimate goal of a united Oneida Nation, one which, unfortunately, had its existence disrupted by the Revolution. Common causes, such as a shared ancestry, language, national experience, territory, and culture, were insufficient to overcome generations of animosity and suspicion.

The devil who first stewed this contaminated brew was the Reverend Samuel Kirkland, a Presbyterian missionary sent to the Oneidas in 1765 after a failed bid to convert the Senecas to his brand of hellfire and damnation. The Oneidas were beset by internal divisions, primarily between the chiefs and the warriors, prior to Kirkland's arrival.

Many Oneidas had become Catholics and moved to settlements along the St. Lawrence River such as Oswegatchie (near present-day Ogdensburg, New York). A hundred years previously, in 1668, a small band of Oneidas had migrated to the Montreal area, where they settled at La Prairie. They were ultimately absorbed by Catholic Mohawks, who moved the village a number of times before permanently settling at an area southwest of the island of Montreal in a community they called Kahnawake (Caughnawaga), or "By the Rapids."

Kirkland found the Oneidas open to his emotionally charged preaching. He allied himself with Christian converts such as Skenandoa (Shenandoah) and Agwerondongwas ("Good Peter") but made enemies of the traditional, or pagan, Oneidas. His views were firmly wedded to the American rebels, and he was emphatic about securing the support of many Oneidas to their cause. The result of his manipulations was a chronically fractionalized Oneida Nation incapable of making any formal declarations for peace or war. But enough Oneidas lent their military and intelligence-gathering skills to the Americans to not only paralyze the Grand Council, but to secure a U.S. victory at Saratoga, the most critical battle of the entire war.

Afterward, Kirkland rewarded himself by securing large tracts of land for himself and his friends by engaging in a series of cessions he knew were controversial. Kirkland sought to temporize some of these thefts by establishing Hamilton College in Clinton, New York, an institution that was, by its charter, meant to provide for the formal educational needs of Oneidas and the surrounding communities.

Kirkland's legacy after his death in 1808 was an Oneida people ready to tear each other apart over religious and political differences. Even as the land was being stolen from under their feet, they could not muster sufficient consensus to form a united stance, hence the ease with which most of them elected to leave the region for distant Wisconsin.

But it took another corrupt preacher, this time the Episcopalian Mohawk deacon Eleazer Williams of Akwesasne, to make the relocation actually happen. Like Kirkland, Williams arrived at Oneida during a time of great unrest in the year 1816. Driven from Akwesasne because of his spying activities for the United States during the War of 1812, Williams ingratiated himself with the Oneidas even as he was planning to fulfill one of Thomas Jefferson's goals: removing all Natives west of the Mississippi.

Williams had a personal stake in the relocation of the Oneidas. Not only was he receiving bribes from land companies engaged in the stealing of Iroquois territory, but he believed that once the Oneidas were settled in Wisconsin, he could use them to become the grand chief of all Native nations in the upper Midwest. Williams also had some people convinced he was the "Lost Dauphin" of France, the son of the beheaded Louis IX who had been confined in prison and then died under unexplained circumstances. Many royalists believed the boy was taken from Europe and left in the care of friendly Mohawks. Despite William's Native features, he was the subject of serious inquiry as to his claims of royal blood, which were never proven beyond doubt.

For many Oneidas a move to Wisconsin provided temporary relief from internal tensions, but not long after they arrived in Green Bay, the passions of their respective beliefs once again tore at them, causing some to petition to the United States to move even farther west.

The Oneidas who elected to stay in central New York did not fare well. Large chunks of their territory were lost to them as they were bribed, coerced, and lied to by state officials responsive not to the law, but to the speculators who were making them rich. The Holland Land Company, the Ogden family, the Peter Smith clan, and even John Jacob Astor took turns at the Oneidas, each growing wealthy at the expense of a beaten people.

Another group, the traditionalists, or pagans, called it quits in New York when they used their resources to buy a reserve along the Thames River in western Ontario. They moved in 1840, taking most of the remaining 600 or so Oneidas left in what was once a land base that stretched from the St. Lawrence to the Susquehanna. The Marble Hill group, consisting of a few Christian Oneidas and those who lived at Onondaga, were all that remained of the Standing Stone People, the children of the men who shed their blood for the American patriotic cause.

There are specific rituals within Haudenosaunee culture for healing individual, familial, communal, and national sufferings. These acts of condolence specifically address the cause of the misery and, through the use of prayers, music, and spiritual offerings, effect reconciliation and healing. Forgiveness and restoration of *kanikenriio*, the "good mind," is stressed as a person who is unburdened by hate may then apply reason and clarity of thought toward the resolution of the matter that has provoked grief or hostility.

Condolence speeches are an integral part of traditional Iroquois funeral services, when the speaker addresses both the surviving kin and the spirit of the departed. Some of the more elaborate of all Iroquois rituals are the condolence ceremonies connected with the death of a chief and the installation into office of his successor. These events take a full day to complete and are characterized by songs and speeches as preserved by the Haudenosaunee from the formation of the Confederacy to present times.

By pooling the emotions of the nations assembled to take part in the condolences, the people as a whole are restored to *kanikenriio* and are thereby able to assume their normal duties. Without *kanikenriio* they will remain confused, blinded by tears, unable to speak, and deaf to the world around them.

This is what happened to the Oneida before, during, and after the American Revolution. Their chiefs had fallen, but before they could be replaced, and the nation renewed, the warrior and the Christian faction interfered, preventing the seating of a working national council that may have well deterred Kirkland's antitraditional manipulations and prevented the young men from going to war against their Iroquois kin. If the Oneida Nation had stood with the Confederacy, it may well have held on to most of its aboriginal lands and prevented the move to the west.

In 1986 the Oneidas made their way back to Onondaga, but there was no peace in their minds. The Southwold group had been sending their traditional leaders to Onondaga for many years to insure their interests were addressed, but without having a land base in the homelands they were subject to challenges from the New York State–based Oneidas.

What is truly ironic is that those who claimed to speak on behalf of the New York Oneidas could only sustain their standing as Oneida because their immediate ancestors had elected to leave Southwold to return to their home territory. Plus, the only Oneida governing entity who could claim to be the proper inheritors of an unbroken administrative line were, again, the traditional council from Southwold.

In the 1970s the U.S. Bureau of Indian Affairs (BIA) had established a formal policy for "recognizing" Native governments. There are seven cardinal standards a Native council must meet to have their land base acknowledged as "Indian country" while qualifying for federal assistance. These include recognition on a continual, unbroken basis; evidence that the group is descended of those who historically inhabited a specific area; existence of a entity that has exercised jurisdiction over its members throughout history; a governing set of laws; a list of all members past and present; exclusive membership in the group that seeks recognition; and proof the group was not terminated by Congress.

The weakest link in the Oneida chain has been the continual, "throughout history" sections of the recognition process. Without standing as acknowledged by the BIA it would be very difficult for a Native government to sue the United States or other entities for loss of land. In the 1970s the Oneidas did have an agency that claimed to speak on their behalf in the homeland area, but it was subject to constant challenges from the factions which continued to plague the people.

At one time the BIA tried to have the matter as to who speaks for the homeland Oneidas resolved through secret ballots, only to have the voting interrupted when the ballot box was stolen in front of government officials.

Also of concern was the lack of a territorial base for the Oneidas. By the 1920s, there was only the 32-acre tract remaining as Indian country as defined by the United States, and only one family resided on the land. In the early 1960s Maisie Shenandoah, the daughter of Mary Cornelius, moved to the territory, soon to be followed by her twin sister, Elizabeth. Other Oneidas, and a few Mohawks, drifted to the 32 to live in trailers supplied by the U.S. government.

Maisie Shenandoah was selected as the clanmother by the Wolf Clan, but finding her male counterpart to assume the duties as chief was difficult. There were few Oneida speakers left in the region, an essential requirement to become a chief since that person was expected to conduct the monthly ceremonies which mark the traditional, or longhouse, calendar.

Also a problem was the behavior of the Oneida men who had returned to the 32 acres. The small reservation developed a sad reputation for violence and substance abuse. The most tragic example was the May 1981 murder on the territory of a 21-year-old former college student named Tammy Mahoney. The local police had traced her movements to the territory and were certain she was assaulted, then killed, and allegedly, her remains are buried somewhere on or near the 32 acres. The police were also sure they knew who was involved in her murder, but the ring of silence could not be broken.

Questions arose as to what the Oneidas knew about the Mahoney murder and why such a crime would be tolerated by the territory residents as it was fairly common knowledge as to who was involved. For those Iroquois who believed in the ancient ways the failure to resolve the agony felt by Ms. Mahoney at the instance of her death would have enormous ramifications for the Oneidas. There would be severe consequences for everyone involved, manifested in such ways as drunkenness, violence within families, mental illness, and disharmonies within the community as a whole. The peace desperately needed by the Oneidas to unify would be evasive as long as the Mahoney spirit was caught between this world and the next. She would not be free until properly mourned, nor would the Oneidas know peace until they had reconciled with her family.

There was another aspect to the Mahoney murder which was understood and feared by the Iroquois. We believe those who die discard the physical shell but have spiritual substance which has awareness. Most people make the transition into the spirit world knowing the change is taking place. They leave this dimension with only moderate ripples. Then there are those who are torn violently from their bodies, particularly accident victims and those whose lives are ripped away because of murder. Particular attention is given to these kinds as their confusion can be used to adversely influence the living.

Traditional Iroquois watch closely for those who are overly ambitious, envious, malicious, or greedy for power and wealth. Because they are insecure, suspicious, and emotional, they are psychologically vulnerable and may be affected by hostile spiritual beings. It is also believed there are those who can manipulate spiritual confusion into real physical power by using the spirits to sow discord among their opponents or by causing accidents, illnesses, and deaths.

The Oneidas have been closely watched to see how they were affected by the Mahoney killing. Would they use it to compel secrecy among their small group or cause fear in those who might otherwise speak about what they knew?

In 1986, there were rumors, bad ones, about the wild parties on the 32 acres. Despite this, the Grand Council of the Haudenosaunee made an effort to reach out to the Oneidas there. In 1986 the Confederacy acknowledged three men as having the task of presenting the concerns of the Oneidas to the Grand Council and then reporting back the results to the Oneidas.

These three were not governmental officials, nor did they wield any administrative authority. They were to attend the Grand Councils and other meetings until such a time as the Oneidas were prepared to restore a governing council of chiefs, clanmothers, and faithkeepers. The only way this could be done was in concert with their Oneida kin from Ontario.

At the 1986 Grand Council this suggestion did not sit well with the homeland Oneidas, who, by that time, were running a highly successful commercial bingo operation and tobacco stand. They were apprehensive about sharing their new wealth with other Oneidas. Some of them also realized a traditional council would, by virtue of its adherence to Iroquois belief, have to take a stand against commercial gambling, which included bingo and other games of chance.

The animosity among the Oneidas was visible since they found it uncomfortable to sit together as a group. At previous sessions they were asked to caucus outside of the longhouse and, at times, had reached consensus on some issues. When it became obvious the Oneida issues on the agenda would soon degenerate into accusation and recriminations, the Oneidas were asked once again to retreat into caucus. This time, there was no meeting of the minds. They informed the Council that despite hours of effort, they could not agree on issues such as the land claims, jurisdiction, economic development, or anything else. Any opportunity for unification evaporated at that Grand Council, to be followed by armed standoffs, fist fights, occupations, and the dynamiting of the 32-acre bingo hall in 1988, involving some members of the Southwold community.

As an editor, I received calls from one faction of the Oneidas pleading for the Mohawks to send aid in their defense. This request was passed on to the Mohawk Nation, but the crisis on the 32 acres was beginning to ebb with the intervention of U.S. authorities and the subsequent conviction of those who had executed the explosions in the bingo hall.

My next experience with the Oneidas took place in late 1990, when Mohawk Nation Chief Jake Swamp and I visited the 32 acres. We were welcomed by Maisie Shenandoah in a manner befitting a clanmother whose home is, by custom, open to all. With Maisie was her daughter, Joanne, a computer company executive who had just moved home after a few years in Washington, D.C.

Once I met Joanne, my personal destiny shifted. We courted long distance and married in Hawaii ten months after my first visit. I continued my work as editor for another year, then made the decision to adhere to Iroquois tradition by leaving Akwesasne to live on my wife's territory among her family. Joanne and I have lived within Oneida territory ever since.

While my observations about the Oneidas may have been casual prior to 1991, they became serious in the years that followed. Of the three Oneida spokespersons in 1986, two had died, and the one remaining decided to change his status from messenger to the head of a council he had fabricated from bits and pieces of Oneida culture. An entity called the "men's council" was designed and imposed upon the 32-acre Oneidas in 1993. By no mere coincidence, the council came into being at the same time as a highly secretive casino gambling compact was signed between the newly minted Oneida "representative" and New York Governor Mario Cuomo. In a deal that was truly bad for New York the Oneidas could build a casino and tender nothing to the State. At no point were the Oneida people informed about the compact, nor have they ever endorsed its provisions, yet the casino was up and running by August 1993 in a building which they had been told was a new bingo hall but which was architecturally designed as a casino.

The duplicity continued. The Oneida people never held an assembly to empower a men's council, which has no basis in Iroquois law. At a hearing held at a Grand Council at Onondaga in late April 1993 the members of the men's council were asked how they came to be.

Their response was that they had been hand picked by the Oneida Nation representative Ray Halbritter, in breach of every democratic tradition held sacred by the Haudenosaunee. The title "representative" was unique among the Iroquois because no governing entity had ever made use of the term. The question before the assembly at Onondaga was to discuss what a representative did and for whom. No single person could, under traditional law, claim to be the singular voice of an entire nation, hence a representative was without legal merit. The Haudenosaunee also concluded that *to represent* did not necessarily mean *to govern*. None of the members of the men's council met the minimal qualifications for leadership as set by custom, but their lack of standing did make them ideal candidates for manipulation. Because they lacked the cultural knowledge traditional chiefs or clanmothers must possess, the men's council had no basis to challenge anything the representative did, nor did they have standing to appeal to the Grand Council since they possessed neither wampum nor title.

The Grand Council reconvened in August 1993 to demand the U.S. federal government acknowledge its decision to strip the Oneida representative of his meager position as messenger. Since the Grand Council placed him in that position, an action endorsed by the BIA in 1986, it also had the authority to remove him. The BIA agreed with the Grand Council—the Oneida representative had lost his federal standing.

The reaction by the representative was swift. He had the support of the two New York senators and the local U.S. congressman. After a flurry of activity the head of the BIA was ordered to reverse the decision and reinstate the representative the very next day.

A few weeks later, the BIA received a package which was said to be the governing rules of the men's council of the Oneida Nation of New York, a hastily drafted document which is very loosely based on Iroquois law. Despite urgings to the contrary, the BIA caved in to the pro-gambling interests in New York and granted formal recognition to the men's council of the Oneida Nation of New York, a descriptive phrase which, despite its inherent contradiction, has never been seriously challenged.

There were, however, many Oneidas in upstate New York who refused to acknowledge the men's council. They wanted a government that adhered to the Great Law, one that would bring about the unification of the Oneida people as envisioned by Mary Cornelius Winder and many others. These Oneidas challenged the authority of the men's council, as they were obligated to do if they were to respect the decision of the Grand Council. For this they endured years of hostility and oppression without significant external support, with the exception of local human rights groups and the legal assistance of the Center for Constitutional Rights in New York City.

The business operations of the Oneida Nation of New York continued to expand virtually unchecked throughout the 1990s. Local ordinances were ignored, as were federal laws protecting sensitive ecosystems, in the rush to expand the casino into an all-inclusive resort complex. A series of gas stations were built which also marketed tobacco products at prices significantly lower than tendered by non-Native retailers. In response, lawsuits were filed and appeals made to state and federal officials, but to no avail. The gambling operations of the Oneida Nation were generating hundreds of millions of dollars in profits which were, under the provisions of the National Indian Gaming Act, supposed to be earmarked for services to the Oneida people. But when some Oneidas sought an accounting as to the funds made on their behalf, they were informed by the National Indian Gaming Commission that such data were classified.

In 1996 the Gaming Commission did threaten to order the Oneida's Turning Stone Casino closed for failure to provide it with an accounting of its finances, to which the Oneida Nation responded, but after a decade of gambling the Oneida people had not received a forensic audit of the money generated using their collective status.

In response to the pro-Confederacy activities of some Oneidas, the men's council created the second largest "Native" police force in the United States. Over 50 non-Native agents, many of whom were former members of the New York State Police, were hired to patrol the 32-acre territory and the casino grounds. Most Oneidas were thoroughly intimidated by this massive show of force, with their fears compounded by the creation of an Oneida Nation court system which was run by non-Native judges, whose laws were drafted by non-Native lawyers with no background in Iroquois culture.

The Oneida Nation court went so far as to exempt the men's council from having to abide by its rulings while in their official capacity. Since the Oneida Nation did not have a jail, any Native person detained by its police was transported 350 miles away to a holding facility in Cambria County, Pennsylvania, as no county in New York State recognized the arresting authority of the Nation's officers.

When the critics of the Oneida Nation refused to be silenced, the men's council issued directives which stripped them of their membership benefits for a series of what it called "treasonous" acts, including meeting with Oneidas from Wisconsin and unnamed "Canadians." No independent hearings were held—a simple allegation was sufficient to have the accused placed at risk.

A second tactic was to enact a secretive housing code, which was then applied subjectively to the few remaining families on the 32 acres. Most of the mobile homes were bulldozed and the residents relocated to a U.S. federally subsidized housing project, where they were compelled to live under intense surveillance by the Oneida Nation police. Resistance to the housing code brought carloads of enforcers to insure the eviction orders were carried out. The Oneida Nation police carried their firearms openly, despite their murky legal status as legitimate officers.

Criminal investigations, particularly that of the Tammy Mahoney case, were impossible to conclude because the Oneidas refused to give sensitive information to the local district attorney, knowing the incestuous relationship between the New York State Police, the county sheriff, and the Nation's police was shared, meaning any potential informant was at high risk.

In the first decade of the twenty-first century the legal tactics of the traditional Oneidas were sufficient to keep the Oneida Nation's bulldozers on hold. Appeals were made to the U.S. federal courts and, finally, to the U.S. Supreme Court to compel the Oneida Nation to abide by the provisions of the 1968 Indian Civil Rights Act, which, the plaintiffs argued, had been systematically breached by the defendants.

Relations between the Oneida Nation of New York and its Ontario and Wisconsin relatives deteriorated quickly once commercial gambling began in earnest. Public statements condemning the "Wisconsins" were issued by the representative whenever the land claims were approaching resolution. The Oneida Nation of New York felt sufficiently secure to completely disregard the Grand Council, then created havoc within the Confederacy by offering $2 million to the Cayugas as a business loan. The result was the dissolution of the Cayugas as a united people since many of them vehemently opposed commercial gambling or taking money from the Oneida Nation, which was an obvious tactic to further weaken the Confederacy as a unit.

Perhaps humans do not change their basic characteristics over time. The Oneida experience is intriguing because they are once again in a position to inflict a terrible blow against the Haudenosaunee. Their decision to defy traditional law and ignore the needs of the collective, to play into the hands of New York State officials and to exchange their homelands for monetary, and momentary, gain, is precisely what happened before, during, and after the American Revolution.

The problem for the Haudenosaunee as a whole is that whatever fate befalls the Oneidas also awaits the other Iroquois nations. By failing to heed the warnings of history, the Haudenosaunee are now condemned to repeat it.

CHAPTER 8

∾

Akwesasne Collapse

The time was 9:30 P.M. on April 30, 1990. Thirteen men gathered at the home of David George, Jr. on the Quebec side of the Akwesasne reservation to welcome, against great odds, the morning of May 1, 1990. The home is on the banks of the Adirondack-born St. Regis River, which snakes its way through hills, marshes, and forests before emptying its blackish brown waters into the sweeping cold green flow of the St. Lawrence 100 meters north of the George home.

Eleven of the men are Native, including Richard "Cartoon" Alford, a direct descendent of Tecumseh, a Shawnee born in Oklahoma and a naturalized member of the Mohawk Nation's Turtle Clan. He is a cofounder of the Oklahoma chapter of the American Indian Movement, a veteran of the Wounded Knee takeover in 1973, and a survivor of many conflicts with armed opponents ranging from street gangs to federal marshals. His emotions are controlled and directed. He'll be the squad leader as the group stands ready to defend the George home, waiting for the attack they know is imminent.

The men are about to take part in the most intense gun battle on Canadian soil since the Louis Riel uprising in Saskatchewan 120 years previous. And in doing so, they will defeat an American-based invasion of Canada while the famed Royal Canadian Mounted Police stand aside, waiting to count bodies. The Mohawk men were drawn to the George home, determined to make a stand against the outlaw groups which had come to dominate the lives of the Mohawk people, groups which solicited money, narcotics, and weapons from organized crime to fund and operate 13 casinos, none of which was licensed or regulated by any government.

They knew the leaders of the assault force brought to bear against them were prepared to take physical control over the entire reservation, but what the defenders did not suspect was the larger plan: to consolidate power at Akwesasne before launching an attack on Onondaga, the capital and spiritual center for the Haudenosaunee.

The defenders had witnessed the dissolution of Native control over the 28,000-acre reservation, the only aboriginal community dissected in half by the Canadian–U.S. border, a problem made worse when officials in Washington and Ottawa empowered colonial administrations of limited authority to oversee the delivery of governmental services while offering severely limited self-rule to the Mohawks. Excluded from real power was the ancestral Mohawk Nation Council, which never abandoned its assertion to complete jurisdiction over all of Mohawk territory, but without formal recognition the Nation Council was restricted to maintaining the collective spiritual rituals which have been a part of Iroquois life for hundreds of generations.

The pro-gambling elements at Akwesasne exploited these divisions with as much ease as a federal bureaucrat. Many of the casinos were owned by Mohawk individuals who bragged about the huge amounts of money they had made through the smuggling trade. They had openly, proudly, taken goods across the border, carrying whatever product turned the highest profit. Cigarettes from the United States were bought in bulk and hauled by the tractor trailer load to dropping off places on the reservation; some of the smugglers had warehouses crammed with cases, while others stuffed the goods in basements and garages. The loads were broken down into smaller units, which were placed aboard fast-moving boats and taken across the St. Lawrence to Cornwall Island on the Ontario side of Akwesasne before being carted to markets in Ottawa, Montreal, and Toronto. The profits were huge.

Still other smugglers carried smaller cargoes; some specialized in narcotics, while others preferred to traffic in human beings. These activities carried a higher degree of risk, both from the police and the organized gangs in Canada, but the money was higher. It had become fairly common for Mohawk homeowners along the St. Lawrence to see boats heavy with product skimming at high speed to make a delivery or to hear late-night water traffic whine to the U.S. shores. They knew the midnight runners, using night vision scopes, were the most likely to carry dope and refugees. Knowing this, and also realizing the runners had sufficient firepower to rip apart any police agency that challenged their operations, the Mohawks stood by, helpless, desperate, and fearful.

The smugglers had become casino owners, despite the opposition of the Mohawk leadership. They had been condemned in the fall of 1986 when the first slot machines showed up at the Bear's Den Truck Stop in the center of Akwesasne. The three Mohawk councils combined forces to seek the peaceful removal of the slots, only to have their notices tossed aside. Appeals were made to the U.S. authorities to remove the slots, which were being trucked in from Las Vegas, Nevada, across many state lines, an action which was in violation of U.S. federal law. Other than a couple of half-hearted, and thereby ineffective, raids by the FBI, the games continued without any serious breaks. Many Mohawks had suspected that the New York State Police had been compromised by the casino operators, with troopers seen in the company of some of the gambling hall owners. The Mohawks knew an FBI raid was coming when the casinos started taking out their machines and hiding them in barns throughout the reservation before the agents arrived. Someone was giving the casino owners inside information, so suspicion fell on the troopers. Having a former member of the state police act as a cash delivery man in his armored truck did nothing to allay their doubts as to the integrity of the troopers, most of whom were from the northern New York region.

The 13 casinos at Akwesasne made it the largest gambling site in the United States outside Nevada and New Jersey. The slot machines were said to have been fixed to minimize payouts. While slots in other jurisdictions may have had, by law, to pay out up to 90 percent, the Akwesasne games did just the reverse. Options were available for regional non-Native investors. In an area of perpetual poverty the appeal of making easy, undeclared money was hard to resist. Potential investors were lured to the casinos by pitching to them the possibility of owning their own slot machine. By "buying" a machine for $1,500, the "owner" received a percentage of the take, with the balance going to the house.

Questions arose as to where the slot machines came from and how it was possible to openly transport the unlicensed devices across state lines. The Mohawks did their own investigating when the FBI refused to take their complaints seriously. They learned the slots came from a company in New Jersey, which shipped them to Las Vegas, Nevada, before they were carried in the trucks of a Massena, New York, transport company to the reservation. The machines were warehoused in a building west of Akwesasne, then taken to the casino that had placed an order. The machines came from a New York City–based Mafia organization which also operated in Nevada, a fact uncovered by the Canadian Broadcasting Company's (CBC) "Fifth Estate" investigating program. The CBC journalists used a hidden camera while they investigated one Mafia member, who readily acknowledged the Mohawk connection while praising the Native owner of the largest casino on the reservation.

The Mafia was able to enter Akwesasne by supplying slots because of its business connections with at least one casino owner. This person was Mohawk but had left home while a teenager to earn a living as an ironworker in the northeast and Midwest. It was believed he had made his first connection with the Mafia while on the job in Cleveland, Ohio. The mob was looking for someone from a minority group to serve as a front for the submission of building contracts in Ohio, which the Mohawk agreed to do. He was given lucrative kickbacks, then later served his bosses by acting as a middleman when the Mafia sought to infiltrate casino gambling among the Native rancherias in southern California. Flush with cash and connections, the Mohawk man returned to Akwesasne to take part in the tobacco smuggling trade, while building his own casino along the Route 37 strip.

With the casinos came other activities that alarmed many Mohawks. Stimulants such as cocaine and its crack derivative were easily available to the casino workers. Some said they had the option of taking their pay in either cash or coke, with many preferring coke. Liquor, long a scourge among the Mohawks, was easily obtainable, and rumors about Native girls being lured into prostitution were common. An increasingly heavy traffic burden clogged reservation roads as tour bus operators brought in customers by the thousands. It was clear none of the patrons cared that the casinos were in violation of U.S. and Mohawk laws or that the community was being shredded by dissension, discord, and corruption. The gamblers would come onto the reservation despite the protesters, police raids, or rocks hurled at the large buses which carried them from Syracuse, Toronto, Ottawa, and Montreal.

The public sessions at the community centers in the village of St. Regis (on the Canadian side) and in Hogansburg (in the United States) became heated whenever the issue of gambling was on the agenda. The casino operators sent in their employees to argue that gambling brought in money to an area which was the poorest in New York State. The collapse of the mining, fishing, and lumber industries a generation ago had caused many Mohawks to enter the ironworking trade, an activity which required them to leave home for weeks at a time. The jobs they found paid well, but much of that was consumed by having to live in expensive urban areas, while the long drives to and from the reservation whittled away more of their wages. Ironworking could also be a seasonal occupation, one in which there might be months of unemployment.

The absence of the male parent meant that women raised the children, organized community events, and took local jobs for extra income. Since the males often left school just after, or prior to, high school graduation, the women took advantage of federal education programs by attending local colleges. They used their formal skills to manage communal services ranging from health care delivery to serving as teachers in the reservation schools.

Mohawk women also exercised another ability—that of becoming political leaders. They campaigned for, and won, offices as chiefs in both the St. Regis Tribal Council and the Mohawk Council of Akwesasne. They were also the most adamant in their opinions about gambling, both for and against. Creating jobs at Akwesasne to keep the men home was a persuasive argument to keep the casinos open, but equally emphatic were women concerned about the rise in crime, its attendant violence, and the moral corruption of Mohawk children. As social workers, nurses, substance abuse counselors, and emergency medical technicians, Mohawk women saw the grim effects gambling was having on the community, but with limited resources and a fractionalized Native government, there was no clear remedy.

Traditional conflict resolutions were tried by the antigambling Mohawk women. They made appeals to their leaders, but without a singular policing agency the rules against commercial gambling passed by popular referendum or through the clans simply could not work. Appeals to external agencies such as the FBI were dangerous since those who advocated these measures were accused of undermining Mohawk jurisdiction. In 1985 and 1986 the voters for the Tribal Council placed into power two women as part of the three-person Tribal Council. In 1987 a third moderate was elected with the same core support, but these three leaders could not stop the explosion of casino gambling. They could try to persuade other Mohawks from bringing slot machines to the reservation, but without a strong police force they could do nothing to stop the flow of gambling devices into the area.

Frustrations rose throughout the fall and winter of 1989–1990. The unity movement initiated by the three Mohawk governments at Akwesasne had stalled when one of the two female tribal chiefs was defeated in an extremely narrow vote in June 1988, while the second female chief chose not to run for reelection. In their place were two firm advocates of gambling. Those two decided there was a need to endorse the creation of a paramilitary gang, which would be used to intimidate internal gambling opponents while threatening the U.S. officials with armed defiance if any attempt was made to interfere with the casinos. This group, called the Mohawk Sovereignty Security Force

(MSSF), held sophisticated firearms in excess of anything possessed by the New York State Police. They were blunt in their defiance of U.S. federal or state laws: enter Akwesasne, and get ready to fight.

The MSSF was led by convicted smugglers and was financed by the casinos. Its members were ill disciplined, violent, and confrontational. They were given machine guns but received no formal military or police training. They used broad slogans that provided the external media with striking images of Mohawk "warriors" willing to die for a noble cause, but they were seen by the Akwesasne residents as an organized gang of thugs, most of whom were involved in committing crimes against the very people they said they were protecting. It was clear the only reason their opponents were not shot outright was the hesitancy to spill the blood of a relative, and most residents of Akwesasne were deeply intertwined with each other genetically, through marriage or by clan.

The antigamblers saw the reluctance of the MSSF to commit its power to crush opposition as an opportunity to remove the threat, and fear, altogether. Almost all of those who carried firearms for the MSSF were males. They were fathers, brothers, and sons of Mohawk women. In the late winter of 1990, after weeks of machine guns being fired at night, high-speed car chases, threats, fistfights, and heated arguments at public gatherings, the Mohawk women used their influence to try to resolve the tensions before someone was shot. They urged their male partners to attend emergency community meetings, where grievances could be aired and resolutions arrived at.

During one session at the community center in the Akwesasne district of Kanatakon the men from both sides of the gambling issue met to find a way out of the impending crisis. Guided by a common concern for their shared Mohawk heritage, the men from both sides of the gambling issue spoke of their fears that unless some kind of solution was realized at that specific time, the sporadic clashes would become more organized, with the strong possibility that some of those in the meeting hall would become victims.

It was unusual for Mohawk men to speak bluntly about their doubts and to do so with emotion. Each man who desired to stand and speak was heard with patience and without interruption. They talked about families afraid to leave their homes at night, of relatives who refused to address each other in public, and of teenagers driven to distraction and drink because of the tensions around them. It had become far too easy to hate those on the other side, yet when they saw their kin at that late March meeting, there was a palatable sense of relief that other than a few bruises and cuts from fistfights, the viciousness of an automatic firearm had not torn apart bodies and souls.

The session continued for some hours, with the women waiting outside. Selecting spokesmen from among their groups, the men agreed to form a joint committee which would urge all Akwesasne residents to put aside their weapons and submit their complaints to the central group, which would in turn seek peaceful resolutions binding on everyone. The MSSF would disband and give its support to the joint committee. The gambling issue itself would be put aside until peace was returned to the reservation. The MSSF said they had to take this plan to its leadership but were confident that once again, the dissolution of the community had been avoided. There would be no need to exact blood revenge.

Many of the men decided to stay at the meeting hall to await the approval of the peace plan by the MSSF leaders. They were taken by surprise when they received word that not only was the peace offering rejected, but it was outright condemned with the vilest of profanities. The MSSF leaders were outraged that their members, the men whom they had paid, armed, and drugged, were making decisions which could well affect their casino and smuggling operations without their consent. Those left inside the hall were shocked by the vehemence with which their compromise plan was dismissed. From that time on the Mohawks knew they had to take direct action to resolve the gambling crisis, but given the fact that not one of the three governing councils was prepared to endorse an outright fight, there did not seem to be an apparent, nonconfrontational alternative.

What was to happen next was spontaneous, desperate, and final. It would lead to the 13 men at David George's house, crouched down behind a fieldstone wall, firing at an assault force 10 times their number, keeping the "warriors" at bay as the MSSF crossed into Canada from the United States.

CHAPTER 9

The Warriors

The 11 Mohawk defenders arrived at the George residence to relieve a smaller group of four men who had been in a state of combat for the previous four days. These four had been given up for dead by most other Mohawks, who had listened with growing terror to the gunfire which exploded in rapid bursts from April 27 to the morning of April 30.

WHY GO TO THE RIVER ROAD IN SNYE OTHER THAN TO TAG HUMAN REMAINS?

The standoff at Davey George's residence was a result of the month-long blockade of the central part of the reservation by community residents opposed to the wide-open, uncontrolled casino gambling which had turned a farming-fishing culture into brutal profiteers prepared to protect their games of suspicious chance with assault weapons wielded by a mad-dog, drug-saturated security force.

On March 23, frustrated by the failure of peace negotiations, hesitant leadership, and the lack of decisive action by U.S. law enforcement agencies, the people acted on their own initiative. Without planning beforehand the anti-gamblers set up four roadblocks to deny access to Akwesasne to all casino patrons. They soon discovered they did not have the personnel to effectively control all four of the barricades, first retreating to three, and then to two central blockades located three miles apart on New York State Route 37, the main highway into Akwesasne.

The decision to seal Akwesasne came as a surprise to many, including myself. I was in Syracuse, New York, a three-hour drive south, buying car parts and found out that the diplomatic efforts had completely failed when I was on my way back home. There would be severe ramifications, I thought, as I listened to radio news broadcasts. Many casino employees saw this as a food, home, and clothing issue—they were not about to surrender their jobs without a struggle. And they had the guns.

When I arrived at the headquarters of the Akwesasne Police, located about 150 meters north of the international border in the village of St. Regis, I was told there was serious trouble at one of the three remaining blockades, the one on a side road in the Frogtown district at the southern edge of the American side. Some of my brothers (there are nine besides myself) were said to be in the middle of a standoff which, given their willingness to take risks, was natural. So, too, was my response: to rush to their defense.

I drove straight to Frogtown, with nothing to defend my relatives or myself. In the narrow cone of my headlights I saw a large crowd, vocal, angry, and carrying bats and clubs. I did not see any of my relatives or friends, who, I learned later, were making a fast retreat from the barricades on the other side of the mob. The hay bales and flimsy boards used to form the road barrier were being torn apart by the mob. When I was spotted by the mob, they yelled, cursed, raised their clubs, and started running at my small car. The car had a manual transmission, which I used to make a harsh shift into reverse, blindly racing backward as fast as the engine would go. A few hundred meters north of the barricades, I saw a driveway, which I screeched into, still in reverse, trying not to stall. I then slammed the transmission into first gear and raced back to the police barracks, leaving the mob far behind.

The next month was characterized by incidents of this kind. The two main barricades remained intact, but the occupiers had to endure drive-by shootings, physical assaults, and constant verbal threats. Four weeks of harsh weather followed, wavering between intense cold and bitter, heavy rains. Normally, many Mohawks would have been preparing their fields for the spring plantings, taking part in the fish runs, or cleaning their homes after a long winter, but in 1990, all things usual and ritual were set aside in anticipation of a final resolution of the casino crisis.

The actual manning of the barricades was organized and sustained, for the most part, by elders, women, and teenagers. The men provided physical security, but many of them had no choice but to return to their ironworking jobs. The first week was uncertain and terrifying for those at the barricades did not know when they would be driven from their posts. They had faced down a large bulldozer sent by one of the casino operators to demolish the eastern barricade (called the "eastern door"), but the women clasped hands, sang whatever peace songs they could think of, and refused to move. They knew the dozer operator even beneath his bandana mask. As he inched the blade closer to the women, they sang with greater emotion, saturated with fear, but did not move. The operator was being urged to run over the women by a crowd of casino supporters behind and on either side of the machine, but he hesitated to bring injury to the line of unarmed Mohawk mothers, sisters, grandmothers, and aunts. He slowed the dozer, stopped, and after hesitating, retreated, where his mates greeted him with accusations of cowardice.

A couple of times, the barricades were destroyed and set afire without opposition, but they were quickly rebuilt. The days were marked by press interviews, emergency sessions of the three Mohawk councils, and nighttime shootings. A log was kept at each barricade throughout the month. A partial listing of the hundreds of acts of terror from March 23 to April 24 included the following.

March 24:	Warriors smash state trooper windshield.
March 24:	Warrior shoots at Nation Chief's home.
March 25:	Radio CKON receives threat of arson.
March 26:	Warriors shoot at antigambler gas stations, fuel tanks, and at building with young people inside.
March 26:	Warriors drop off fake bomb at Akwesasne Police station.
March 26:	Warriors fire assault weapons at the people.
March 28:	Warriors plant bomb on school bus.
March 31:	Warriors throw Molotov cocktails at Methodist church.
March 31:	Warriors throw Molotov cocktails at Mohawk Council of Akwesasne administration building.
April 2:	Warriors make bomb threat against MCA.
April 7:	Warriors shoot at Nation Chief's home.
April 9:	Police confiscate cigarettes being smuggled by warriors.
April 9:	Warriors shoot at New York State Police.
April 12:	Warriors ram Akwesasne Police cruiser.
April 14:	Warriors issue hit list of over 200 Mohawks.
April 14:	Arrest warrants issued by New York State for 22 warriors on charges ranging from driving while intoxicated (DWI) to criminal possession of a weapon.
April 15:	Warrior fires over 100 rounds near barricades.
April 19:	Warrior gunfire injures woman at barricade.

April 21:   Warriors fire into barricades.

April 22:   Western barricade destroyed by fire, rebuilt.

April 22:   Warriors fire into eastern barricade.

April 23:   Akwesasne Police station attacked by warriors using firearms, Molotov cocktails, and rocks.

April 23:   Akwesasne Cultural Center gutted by fire after warrior attack.

April 23:   School buses, with students, attacked by warriors.

April 24:   Warriors attack western barricade with assault weapons—hundreds of rounds are fired, compelling the people to flee across fields and along the riverbank, where they are shot at as they run.

April 24:   Warriors attack the eastern barricade with automatic gunfire and gas bombs over a 40-minute period. It is abandoned. Over 25 cars are abandoned by the antigamblers at both barricades and set afire. A casino owner hires a crew to remove the shells of the cars and pick up all shell casings.

The demolition of both barricades by the Mohawk Sovereignty Security Force (the "warriors") effectively broke the back of the antigamblers' physical resistance to the casinos. The terror brought to bear against them was cause for hundreds of Mohawks to leave Akwesasne for safety across the St. Lawrence River into Cornwall, Ontario, where they were given emergency shelter by the Canadian government at an education center. Others found safety with relatives as far away as Rochester and Syracuse.

Not all the antigamblers left Akwesasne. The Akwesasne Police endured three more days of shootings before they were ordered to leave the reservation. While en route to Cornwall, some of the boats used to escape were fired upon by MSSF snipers located on three of the islands that separate the Quebec side of Akwesasne from the city.

The reservation was, by April 27, controlled by the MSSF and the casino group, with the exception of small sections in the Snye area and the central part of Cornwall Island, upon which was located the Canada Customs complex and the buildings of the North American Indian Traveling College (NAITC). The NAITC had lost its cultural center, burned in an act of arson on April 23, but it became the communications center for the refugees until the crisis was relieved in June.

The refugees were convinced New York Governor Mario Cuomo had agreed to recognize the pro-gambling leaders as the de facto leaders of a new Akwesasne governing agency, one which was prepared to terminate a long-standing $400 million land claim against the State in exchange for gambling compacts which would formally introduce casinos into revenue-starved New York.

Governor Cuomo had also developed a personal friendship with Art Kakwirekeron Montour, a native of the Kahnawake Mohawk community across the St. Lawrence River from Montreal. Montour was a spokesperson for the Ganienkeh movement, during which an Adirondack Girl Scout camp was occupied as an assertion of aboriginal Mohawk land rights in 1974. Cuomo was then New York's Secretary of State and took charge of negotiations with the Mohawks at Ganienkeh, ultimately persuading them to move to state land near Plattsburgh, New York. Montour met with Cuomo many times before, during, and after the settlement, only to be driven at gunpoint from Ganienkeh in 1981, accused of treason. He purchased a home southeast of Akwesasne and took a lead role in forming the MSSF.

Many Mohawks believed that Governor Cuomo refused to intervene at Akwesasne because of the MSSF's assurances that the incidences of terror were being wildly exaggerated by the media. At one time Cuomo said the "warriors" were not really "shooting at people," which seemed to dehumanize the Mohawks at the barricades. The state police remained on the borders of the reservation, where they could hear the gunfire and see the barricades set to flames, but were ordered to stay out. On the Canadian side of Akwesasne Mike Mitchell, the grand chief of the Mohawk Council of Akwesasne, gave assurances there would be federal intervention by Ottawa, a promise that seemed believable because of the presence of a large unit of the Canadian army then in Cornwall for training purposes. The refugees were also told the American National Guard was en route to restore peace and protect Mohawk homes and businesses.

Neither of these rumors proved to be true. Mohawk homes were open to vandalism or arson. On the afternoon of April 29, only a few antigamblers remained at home. One family preparing to leave was that of my eldest brother, David "Davey" George, Jr., a noted hunter, trapper, fisherman, and mason. He had built his house on the southern banks of the St. Regis River where it meets the St. Lawrence in the Snye section of Akwesasne, a mere 100 meters north of the U.S. border. He and his wife Martha had used a combination of wood and stone in the construction of their single-story home, which had a large stone fence bordering the River Road in the back of the house. Their half-acre plot sloped down to the water and was landscaped with cedars flanking both sides of the house. At the river's edge Davey had placed a large dock jutting into the shimmering brown waters of the St. Regis. Across from his home was St. Regis

Village, its crowded streets capped by the tall steeple of the St. Regis Church, a field stone gray structure 200 years old and built by the Mohawks, including the ancestors of the George family.

Davey had decided to act on the advice of his friends and leave Snye for Cornwall since he had been told the Canadian military was on its way. He did not then know the MSSF had targeted his home to be torched as a warning to anyone considering opposing its takeover of Akwesasne. Abandoning a home he and Martha had designed and built did not sit well with him, so he changed his mind and elected to wait for the promised assistance. Martha went to the refugee center, but Davey, a man truly feared by the MSSF, stayed, intending to defend his home with his hunting rifle and a shotgun.

Miles away from River Road, I was ready to leave Akwesasne with my brothers Dennis and Dean. My work as the editor of two publications to expose the gambling and smuggling operations placed me at risk. The offices of *Akwesasne Notes* and *Indian Time,* the two periodicals I edited, had been torched—twice. We had been boycotted and threatened, our articles intensely scrutinized for inaccuracies or distortions. While our investigative resources were severely limited, I had worked with many journalists to encourage them to not only review the background of the gambling issue, but to apply universal standards of credibility to their sources.

As my brothers and I were packing up emergency clothing and personal effects, we had a visitor. David Leaf, a longtime family friend, told us that Davey had been attacked by the MSSF, and word was that he had wounded one of them. Brushing aside all other concerns, we drove quickly through the back roads of the Snye district to Davey's home. We saw he was highly agitated and had blocked the River Road on either side of his home because he had been threatened by the MSSF. Warning shots had been fired into the air, but no one was hurt. It was impossible to abandon my brother, so we elected to stay until relieved by the Canadian forces.

Besides Davey and I, we had my younger brother Dean, my brother-in-law Cartoon (Tecumseh's descendent), and two other friends. We were armed with a variety of hunting rifles ranging from a 30–06 to a 22/250 bolt action. We also had a couple of shotguns and a semiautomatic AKS rifle, .223 caliber. A .308 rifle was also in the house but was useless since it was without ammunition. With this puny arsenal we made ourselves ready to push back the MSSF attacks. Against us was a gang armed with weapons ranging from Uzis to at least one .50-caliber machine gun, modified Mini-14s, AK-47 automatics, grenades, and a host of handguns.

CHAPTER 10

The Fight

Dusk, April 30, a warm evening, making amends for the past month. The goal of the men was simple: stay alive until relieved, while the tactic was to defend the George property using any and all means necessary. Our group were the descendants of the Mohawk soldiers of generations past, men who had secured for the Haudenosaunee Confederacy dominance over most of the northeast using diplomacy, trade, and unmatched fighting ability.

Their great, great, great grandfathers had come close to breaking the back of American independence 215 years before, while the sons of those men had saved Canada from becoming part of the United States during the War of 1812. Mohawks had picked up weapons and joined the Federal Army not to preserve the Union, but to test their courage in combat. During both world wars, Korea, and Vietnam, virtually all adult Mohawks volunteered for the armed services, where they sought front line duty.

My own father, David George Sr., was a member of the Glengarry Highlanders, a unit of the Third Canadian Army during World War II. He saw action in Africa, Sicily, Yugoslavia, France, Belgium, Holland, and Germany. For three years he was under fire by the Germans. On June 6, 1944, he took part in the D-Day strike in Normandy, landing on Juno Beach before striking into the French interior. Armed with a bolt action .303 rifle, his job was to go head-to-head with German snipers and clear their nests, which they would leave behind when the main army retreated. He was a marksman able to control his fears while at deadly risk.

Each one of us had someone in our family with similar abilities. We were about to endure our own such test. The volunteers were Harvey Arquette, Brian David, Dave Francis, Larry David, Ronald Lazore, Kevin King, Ken Lazore, Joe Lazore, Cartoon, my brother Davey, and me. Others, including my brother Dean, found it impossible to come to our aid until the next morning. Ron Lazore and Cartoon were most familiar with military tactics since Lazore was a former Marine and an officer with the Akwesasne Police and Cartoon had his own background in keeping alive in hostile conditions, having been at the 100-day siege of Wounded Knee in 1973. He knew many of the men opposing us, having organized them into fighting units at Kahnawake and at the Ganienkeh takeover in 1974.

It is the custom among the Mohawks that each man shall determine for himself his willingness to place his life in jeopardy during battle. For those who cannot tolerate the risk, there is ample opportunity to withdraw without shame; this is an unspoken understanding that frees those in combat from having doubts about their comrades. Ron and Cartoon knew this and placed each man according to need and ability. Those with superior eyesight and weapons skills, such as Davey, took their place directly behind the stone wall next to River Road, where we expected the most concentrated assault to take place. The others were shown where they were to lie, keeping prone on the ground until given directions where to concentrate their fire.

I was placed between the road and the river. Ron gave me a very quick summary of how to use an AR-15 rifle as it was the first time I had held such a weapon. My job was to stop any flanking attack along the shoreline and to keep the river clear should we be shot at by the speedboats used by the warriors in their smuggling operations. To do this, I had three clips, each holding 20 rounds of .223 ammunition. All of us had severely limited ammunition, which meant we had to take our time and choose targets with precision. I was told to use the road's pavement by firing along its surface, which would send the bullets in an uncontrolled spin and make the MSSF hesitate to use that lane of attack.

Inside our perimeter was the George house, with its single-line phone now occupied by the two *Canadian Press* journalists. Full darkness at that time of the year came about 8:00 P.M.; on that night a heavy cloud cover retained the day's heat while making it seem as if the sky had moved closer to the earth. The air was still, the river's surface unrippled by the wind. We were apprehensive and alert, nervous but unafraid. Reports in the press in the days after the April 24 destruction of the barricades had some of our leaders chastising Governor

Mario Cuomo while predicting it would take human casualties before he sent in either the National Guard or the state police. While the warriors may have felt they could attack other Mohawks with impunity, we knew they would be extremely reluctant to turn their guns on the non-Native police because of the probability of massive physical retaliation, which, in turn, would harm their gambling and smuggling activities.

We knew this, but Cuomo was enamored of the Mohawk warrior image, as were most reporters. On the surface they fit the ideal of terrible and brave Native combatants willing to take on the might of the invaders to preserve their ancient privileges. It was this stereotype, fostered by a willfully blind media, which would come to cause great harm to all Mohawks in the months and years to come. To us, our opponents were us, blood kin, former pals, men and women with whom we had worked and played, people with whom we had shared our lives and had stood with in times of crisis. They were cousins, brothers, partners swayed by the opportunity to ease the weight of poverty which had been a bitter, humiliating experience for many decades. But these arguments were narrow and self-serving, while deliberately ignoring the social, spiritual, and political consequences of what were, by our own definition, criminal acts.

The challenge confronting the 11 men at the George residence was whether their act of defiance had enough merit to justify the probability of their deaths. How they would respond to a concentrated attack leading to that sad end began 90 minutes after complete darkness, when we were fired upon by a speeding boat while the warriors attempted to crest the small hill to our south. Another wave of gunfire came from the west, behind the large willow tree Davey George had cut down to form a blockade on our right flank. We reacted by firing our weapons in all three directions, forcing the warriors to retreat.

During this opening phase, while the bullets were probing for flesh, I was called to the telephone in the house—our communications people on Cornwall Island told me that Governor Cuomo was on a live talk show in Schenectady, New York, and that if I called the station, I might speak with him. By the time I dialed the number, Cuomo was done, but he just happened to pick up the station phone as he was leaving. He took my call, but not while on the air. I stated as clearly as I could who I was and where I was at that instant. I emphasized the need to have the National Guard enter Akwesasne and restore peace. He responded by saying the situation needed further consideration and hinted I was exaggerating the dangers, at which time I held the telephone outside a nearby window so he could hear the machine guns firing at us. Like others who had attempted to cause him to act, I asked him, just before I terminated the call, whether he needed murdered corpses before he sent in the troops. It was apparent that that is precisely what he wanted, and by the afternoon of May 1, that terrible prediction had come to pass.

We fought on and off for the next few hours. On the scanner we listened to the warrior transmissions and learned that at least one of them had been wounded at the River Road tree barricade. Thereafter, we heard one of the warrior women leaders state with clarity, "the order is shoot to kill," as if they had not already been trying to do so. The *CP* reporters went into the basement of the George home, staying there for most of the night. They were overheard calling the Royal Canadian Mounted Police, pleading with them to send a rescue team to take them off the reservation, that as Canadians they had a right to expect their federal police to save their bodies. Their pleas were denied, even as the residents of Cornwall, across the St. Lawrence and miles from the scene of the battle, came out to their front yards to listen to the gunfire; it had been a long time since the Louis Riel uprising in the distant prairies, and Canadians, safe and insular, were not accustomed to using high-caliber automatic weapons to resolve domestic issues. None of the authorities in Ontario or Ottawa thought to take the U.S. federal government to task for its refusal to prevent a concentrated invasion onto Canadian soil by a U.S.-based militia.

Each one of the 11 Mohawk men at the George home refused to buckle and run. Cartoon and Ron proved adept combat squad commanders, directing return fire, carefully allocating our dwindling supply of ammunition, urging us to make our growing anger known by screaming at the warriors, letting them know we were well, ready, and eager for them to attack. Dave Francis, in particular, lived up to his father's combat bravery in Korea by using the AKS to hold the warriors in place while identifying them by name loud enough for them to hear, then attaching appropriate insults according to their past acts of stupidity.

Cartoon patrolled throughout our defensive perimeter, occasionally firing from an eight-round, 12-gauge Franchi-Brescia riot shotgun. By 1:30 A.M., the gunfire was at its most intense, while we could do little but crouch behind the stone walls and wait to respond with the few bullets left. Cartoon, dressed in complete camouflage, made a single-man rush up the hill from which most of the firing came, armed only with the shotgun. Yelling profanities, he walked calmly toward the warriors, firing rounds from the Franchi-Brescia, a couple of which contained a flame-like flare that, when he fired, lit up the hill in an eerie, colorless flash of cone-shaped light. His actions, which surprised us all, silenced the shooting for a few moments, during which he walked back to the house and slammed the door. A short time afterward, Ernie King, the chief of the embattled and abandoned Akwesasne Police, creeped along a low riverbank for a half-mile, bringing us badly needed ammunition. We'd make it until dawn, at least.

The first brush of a new day was heard rather than seen. There was a noticeable lifting of the air, with small ripples forming on the river's surface. As the clouds slowly broke up, sounds carried farther. We began to distinguish the caliber of the bullets fired at us by their respective speed and tone. A .223 round was fast and had a wasp-style hum; the .308 was slower, with a bee-like buzz as it went over our heads. There was no mistaking the choppiness of an Uzi, a weapon we felt was almost uncontrollable in a gunfight and rather useless given the terrain. But the tripod-based .50-caliber machine gun was something we did not want to be brought against us since we knew the warriors had such a slicing device. Just before sunrise, at around 4:45 A.M., we heard intense gunfire on the far side of the hill, as if the attackers were being caught in an ambush. We also heard a woman screaming from a side road called Smokey Hollow used by the warriors to attack us. The road leads to homes on the far side of the small hill, in a place where there was once a burial mound from hundreds of years ago. The woman's words came after a break in the fight, when individual shots were clearly distinctive. One such shot had been fired at Smokey Hollow, which caused the woman to yell, "Why the hell did you do that?" Evidence during legal proceedings would surface that the murder of Harold "Junior" Edwards took place at that time. He was given emergency aid but died shortly afterward, his body then placed where it was discovered later in the day by a local reporter from the *Massena Courier* newspaper.

We, however, were finally given word that a large group of Mohawks, led by the Akwesasne Police, were brushing aside the urgings of many people at the communications center and coming to our assistance. By the time they arrived in the area, it was fully daylight. Joe Lazore and I took positions to the far east of our line, where we could hear the .50-caliber machine gun finally come into action. The warriors on the hill had directed their attention to our relief force, causing them to leave their vehicles for protection. One of the young men in that party was Mathew Pyke, then 26. Pyke and his partner, Linda Lazore, had brought food supplies to the George residence two days before, but I did not have a chance to visit with them or to express my gratitude. Now, he was crouched behind his truck, armed only with a .22 rifle. The Akwesasne Police were using their radios to inform the communications center as to their situation, conversations which were being recorded. It was at that moment that a barely audible grunt was heard—Pyke was shot in the lower back by a warrior sniper located to his rear on Yellow Island. The response by his comrades was immediate. They loaded him into the bed of a pickup, called for an ambulance, and headed to the nearest U.S. town. As they attempted to leave the Snye area, they were stopped at force of arms by the warriors. Vital moments, during which Pyke was suffering severe internal bleeding, were lost as they argued about getting Pyke the emergency medical help he needed. The truck was finally permitted to leave. A few minutes later, Pyke was transferred to an ambulance and taken to the Alice Hyde Hospital in Malone, New York, only to die four hours later.

We were told of Mathew Pyke's wounding when the relief force arrived at our positions after a gunfight which had, in its remnants, hundreds of brass castings scattered along River Road. We had flushed the warriors from their log bunkers near the crest of the hill a few minutes before, with Cartoon leading the final charge, telling us that we had won and that the hill belonged to us. There wasn't much to be pleased with as we walked back to our perimeter to wait for word on Pyke's condition. A short time later, one of the warriors, a young man named Arthur Yopps, stood near the fallen tree to our west. He was waving a white t-shirt and calling for us, saying he did not want to fight anymore and was surrendering. Yopps was well known to my brother Davey as he was one of the teenagers he would take fishing, teaching him how to hunt and trap. Yopps had no animosity toward anyone in our group. We instructed him to walk slowly toward us since we suspected an ambush. Dave King and Dave Francis met Yopps after making sure no one was hiding behind the nearby homes. Their need for security was critical, so they were extremely alert as I was guarding them from the riverbank. Other than Yopps, there was nothing to cause us alarm.

Yopps was brought to the rear of the George house, next to the road. Roger Mitchell and Steve Lazore, two Akwesasne Police officers, were next to him when I asked him a number of questions. He gave to Officer Mitchell a modified Mini-14 assault rifle and a mounted scope with a 100-round drum clip attached to the breach. He said he was given the rifle by a man whom he did not know but whose first name began with a "B." He said, in response to our questions, that there were many people involved in the attack, some of whom were black men and others white. He told us there were serious wounds among the warriors, which, we later found out, were being treated by a Malone-based doctor at the warrior headquarters in the Racquette River district of Akwesasne.

Yopps was shaking, terrified by what he had endured the past few hours and unwilling to continue the fight against his former friends. He was left sitting on the stone wall to wait for a vehicle to take him to Cornwall Island, where he could tell his story to the police and the press. The two *Canadian Press* reporters had made use of the flight of the warriors to leave the area just before Yopps waved his shirt. His statement would help bring about the arrests of those who gave the orders for the attack. But Yopps never did make it to the communications center. My brother was enraged when he saw Yopps, accusing him of shooting at his home; when Davey fired a single round in the air, Yopps ran back to the west, his feet barely touching the ground. He was chased, but no human alive could have caught him before he disappeared past the fallen tree. The assault rifle he gave to us was later turned over to the Royal Canadian Mounted Police, who later denied having the weapon.

We were concerned about the battle being resumed when night returned. We knew the warriors were pumped up on narcotics and alcohol, stimulants which provided a certain heightened sensory awareness but which also caused the taker to come crashing down, his emotions and physical energy exhausted. This explained, in part, why the warriors ran under the glare of the sun. Once the firing ended, the media arrived. While they were holding interviews, shots came from the hill, but they did cause the reporters to pack up their gear and leave. Shortly afterward, we were told to abandon the area since the Canadian and American police were on their way to Akwesasne.

Three of us remained to load a small boat: Dave Francis, my brother Dean, and I. We were searching for my brother Davey when we noticed a heavyset man walking toward us from the west. This came as a surprise since the warriors had blocked the roads on the U.S. side in the center of the reservation and had refused to let anyone pass through. How this person, clearly non-Native, nervous, out of place, and unarmed, made it through the roadblocks was curious, but we did not have time to think about it: our instructions were to leave immediately. The man was a reporter from Massena. He asked if Davey George was home, but we told him to leave. He said a man was lying on the ground next to a white and red house next to the fallen willow tree. We had cleared the area some hours before—no one had been there, so we thought it was someone from the immediate area, perhaps passed out because of heavy drinking. All our men were accounted for, except for Davey, and the description of the man on the ground and his clothes given by the reporter was sufficient for us to realize that the man was not my brother. We once again told the reporter to leave, fired four warning shots in the air to signal Davey we were retreating to Cornwall Island, then left across the river, prepared to return fire if we were shot at. The boat trip from Snye was a bitterly uneventful one.

CHAPTER 11

∾

The Aftermath

Events after May 1, 1990, were jumbled together. In late afternoon of that date, word came to the communications center on Cornwall Island of the second death as a result of the gunfight—that of Harold "Junior" Edwards, also known as "JR," 32 years of age, a construction worker many of us knew as one of moderate temperament and the least likely person to wield a gun for any purpose.

Edwards lived in the Snye district. He was a former student at the Indian Way School in the early 1970s. The school was an attempt to reinforce Mohawk traditional values in a formal setting, with an emphasis on language and culture. While the school dissolved after a few years, it did inspire other Mohawks to start their own educational institutions, ones which adhered to a curriculum firmly based on an Iroquoian world view. Edwards was among the first students. He is pictured in a book titled *Wampum Belts of the Iroquois* by Tehanetorens (1974) holding a reproduction of the war belt that defines the powers of the military leaders of each Iroquois nation.

It was his killing that attracted the attention of the Surete du Quebec (the police force for that province), while the shooting of Mathew Pyke was largely ignored. There were sufficient statements by the men involved in the Snye fire fight to indicate that Edwards had not only been shot across the border, but had been deliberately moved to the Canadian side to confuse the investigation. None of the warriors were questioned, nor were the New York State Police brought into the interviews. It was that agency, under a 1948 federal law, which was given criminal jurisdiction over Indian lands within the state.

Not until May 13 were any of us aware that the Surete had turned a blind eye to the hard evidence and was planning to arrest our group.

At daylight on May 13, the Surete entered the homes of Davey George, Ken Lazore, Roger Mitchell, and Steve Lazore, the latter two officers with the Akwesasne Police. The four were interrogated at the Snye field headquarters of the Surete, a compound which resembled a small military base patrolled by dozens of cops, including Corporal Marcel Lemay, killed two months later when the Surete entered the Kanehsatake Mohawk territory west of Montreal. It was easy for the Surete to find us because we returned to our homes without doubt or apprehension. Unlike the warriors, we did not hide behind bandanas, face paint, or masks; we stood before the Mohawk Nation unbowed, unafraid to accept the consequences of our actions. After reflection we believed that what we had done would be cited by our descendants with pride.

The Mohawks were taken to the Parthenais, a cube-shaped fortress in the east end of Montreal. At their service was the personal helicopter of Robert Bourassa, the Premiere of Quebec. Once I learned of their arrest, I elected to submit to their questioning, fully expecting to follow the others to Montreal (see the appendix). After a night in a steel-walled cage I was taken before a judge in the town of Valleyfield and charged with second-degree murder. The terms of my bail proved to be extraordinary and made it obvious to me that the Crown attorney had a very weak case. For the first time in Canadian judicial history an accused murderer was allowed to remain free on $10,000 bail while living in an alien country, the United States.

The Crown's case was, as became clear during the preliminary hearing, largely fabricated. Although the hearing was stretched over six months, the coerced statements, botched physical investigation, and lack of any hard evidence persuaded the presiding judge to dismiss the charges at the first opportunity. My harsh statements to the press about the cowardice of the Surete and other police agencies to come to our aid was widely quoted in Canada and isolated me as a target of their investigation. But at the time of my discharge on November 1, 1990, the events of Akwesasne's terrible spring were pushed aside by the July blockade of the Mercier Bridge at Kahnawake and the killing of Corporal Lemay at Oka. What the press refused to investigate was the connection between Akwesasne and Oka, how the terror of the spring sprouted in our sister community 100 kilometers way.

By all accounts, the MSSF, the warriors, had suffered a huge defeat on May 1. Not only were they physically beaten, but also, the arrival of the U.S. police meant their casinos would be shuttered permanently. Smuggling was also curtailed because of the river patrols, and they had been roundly condemned in the press. But they saw a chance to recover by establishing a new base of operations in Oka. Settled by Mohawks and other Native peoples, Kanehsatake had gone about its way somewhat removed from the rapids of Iroquois politics. Its residents were quiet, respectful—quite different in temperament than their Kahnawake and Akwesasne relatives. In March of 1990 they had, as was their way, erected a small roadblock to protest the planned destruction of a wood lot near one of their cemeteries. That act attracted only marginal attention in light of Akwesasne's struggles, but they also had to endure a bitter spring manning the barricade. There were no weapons—no one brandished clubs for the press.

On July 11 the nature of Kanehsatake and Native politics across Canada changed when a band of Akwesasne warriors descended upon Oka with the trunks of their cars full of the same assault rifles they had used at Akwesasne. They were uninvited by the community but intruded at the request of a single person. The response by the Quebec authorities was swift. They would not tolerate a repeat of Akwesasne, nor would they be accused of another act of cowardice. The warrior menace would be crushed by a massive show of force. In the early morning of July 11 the Surete sent in its elite strike team dressed in urban warfare gear to drive the warriors from the Oka woods. Thirty seconds of gunfire and the warriors fled, leaving women and children behind. They also left in their wake Corporal Lemay, suffering a serious bullet wound to the head, from which he died shortly afterward.

Certainly, the attempt by the Mohawks of Kanehsatake to prevent the destruction of the forest was consistent with traditional principles of land stewardship. Too often in the twentieth century had the Iroquois been defeated in their efforts to prevent the alteration of their lands for commercial and recreational purposes. At Onondaga, New York State had displaced a number of Oneida families when it built, over their objections, a water control dam on the south end of the territory. Among the Senecas of Allegheny, the bitterness of being forced from their homes was as raw as when the Kinzua Dam created an artificial lake and flooded their homes in 1965. So, too, with the Tuscaroras when Robert Moses, the megalomaniac engineer of the 1950s, decided to attach the western part of their small reservation to a water reservoir for use by the city of Niagara Falls.

The Mohawks had also suffered a heavy blow to their spirits when Canada and the United States agreed to construct the St. Lawrence Seaway straight through Akwesasne and Kahnawake, thereby enabling ocean freighters to bypass the turbulent river rapids but forever changing the traditional land- and water-based economies of both communities. The Mohawks protested but were not tough enough to stop the bulldozers as dams were set in place to pacify the St. Lawrence River, ship locks constructed to raise and lower the freighters, and massive hydroelectric generating stations placed astride the water to provide cheap power for use by cities and industrial plants. Despite litigation and petitions, the only time the Mohawks were heard was when the Seaway was dedicated in April 1959. To succumb passively to politically connected developers was simply intolerable to a new generation of Mohawks able to make effective use of the press through a show of force.

Law enforcement agencies in both Canada and the United States were uncertain as to how to respond to an organized group of armed Natives, possessing not only, in some instances, superior firepower, but the firm conviction that what they were doing was the right thing. It is one thing to assign a highway patrol unit, like the Surete du Quebec or the New York State Police, to monitor the roads and conduct criminal investigations of a personal nature, and quite another to place them in serious jeopardy by ordering them to attack and disarm an Iroquois paramilitary force on its own turf. That is the fatal mistake made by the Surete's commanders. They lacked the right and the training to invade any Mohawk territory, nor were they given instruction as to the motivations of the people they were sent to arrest.

On the other side, the Kanehsatake protesters were successful in preventing the destruction of the forest, only to have their cause obscured when the warrior group arrived. After the death of Corporal Lemay, all subsequent events were determined by nonresidents who need not feel the full consequences of their actions.

Once the Quebec officials sent in the Surete, the same warriors who had been defeated at Akwesasne hijacked control over both Kahnawake and Kanehsatake. Without prior approval they sealed off sections of both communities, with the blocking of the Mercier Bridge being the most disruptive tactic as it caused massive traffic delays when the commuters from the south shore of Montreal were compelled to take distant alternate routes into the city. The public response was predictable: anger tainted by blatant acts of racism. The press reaction only made matters worse. Reporters once again proved their ignorance of the factors involved in what became known as the Oka crisis by failing to apply objective standards of credibility to their sources or to investigate the backgrounds of those people whom they labeled as freedom fighters. The assault rifles of the warriors were hardly cooled from firing at other

Mohawks at Akwesasne when they were brandished for a blissfully ignorant press at our sister communities.

Within a few hours of the killing of Corporal Lemay, word was being circulated at Akwesasne as to who shot the fatal bullet and how it was done. The information was consistent with the results of the formal investigation some months later. It was widely known where the shooter went after Lemay was struck and that the weapon, a Ruger Mini-14 of .223 caliber, had been disposed of, never to be found by the Surete. After the May 13 arrests at Akwesasne it was hardly surprising that no one would dare speak to the Quebec police for fear of being arrested, confined, and perhaps beaten. Given their extreme anger toward all things Mohawk, the only chance the Surete would have of solving the Lemay case would be purely by chance. There was no sympathy for a police agency that had placed the lives of Mohawk women and children in jeopardy and one that cared so little for the safety of the Akwesasne Police, supposedly their law enforcement comrades, as to abandon them to be murdered by the same group that took Lemay's life.

The situation at Oka and Kahnawake was the major story in Canada during the summer of 1990. A week after it had begun, a group of Mohawks, including myself, went to Ottawa to meet with officials at the Department of Indian Affairs to discuss how to diffuse the crisis. Our suggestions were to put into effect traditional Iroquois diplomatic tactics, beginning with the acknowledgment by the federal government in Ottawa that this was an internal matter that had to be resolved using our own methods. We urged the creation of a team made up of experts in Iroquois law, traditional leaders grounded in the ancient values with a firm background in our spiritual values. This was exactly the team that finally broke the impasse at Kahnawake but was rejected by Ottawa. Since there was enormous press coverage of the events, my feeling was that the federal officials, from the Prime Minister to the Premier of Quebec, were enjoying the camera's glow. Sending in units of the Canadian Army when there were creative alternatives was a bad decision based on political factors—their presence increased tensions and distorted the situation beyond any semblance to the reality of Mohawk life. It empowered the warriors by making them powerful symbols of Native activism, while obscuring their involvement in the undermining of the very Mohawk nationalism they publicly espoused.

The standoff continued well into August before the peace team from the Haudenosaunee Confederacy was able to persuade the residents of Kahnawake to dismantle the barricades. That team consisted of Paul Williams, Oren Lyons, Harvey Longboat, and John Mohawk, all firm advocates for the Confederacy at Onondaga as well as experienced in the intricacies of Iroquois diplomacy and traditional protocol. The Confederate delegates were able to call together Canadian officials and Mohawk representatives from the various factions, not an easy task under normal circumstances and made more difficult by the intense feelings of mistrust among the Iroquois themselves.

Knowing from their own internal sources that the residents of Kahnawake and Kanehsatake were prepared to embrace almost any solution that did not involve confrontation or the entry of the hated Surete into their communities, the Confederate peace team was confident the warriors no longer commanded significant popular support. They effected an agreement by meeting with the Mohawk people directly, listening to their concerns, and securing their trust. Empowered by the community, the peace delegates were then able to persuade Canadian and provincial officials to have the military and police units withdraw, while the various judicial agencies promised not to prosecute those residents who manned the barricades. By late August, the warriors who had sparked the crisis by blocking the Mercier Bridge had retreated from the front lines since they lacked the discipline, organization, and manpower to sustain the barricades. For the Mohawks of Kahnawake it came down to a single question: Was the sealing off of the community justified? Dissension within Kahnawake could no longer be controlled given the disintegration of their food supplies and the severe hardships brought about by the disruption to an economy which was almost entirely based on the service industry. While Quebec commuters could not cross into Montreal, neither were they able to spend money buying the tobacco products that were the key to Kahnawake's material prosperity.

At Kanehsatake the warrior group was having serious problems of its own. The various police and military checkpoints made it difficult to supply the two dozen or so men and women who had retreated from the pine woods to a substance abuse treatment center. The Canadian military's task was far easier logistically than that of Kahnawake given the small area it had to contain. Strands of barbed wire kept the warriors in while preventing them from either interfering with regional traffic or threatening their opponents within Kanehsatake or nearby Oka. When the Kahnawake roadblocks were taken down on August 29, the warrior group at the treatment center was left without any significant bargaining chip. All the Canadian officials had to do was to wait and allow the internal pressures within the warrior group to break it apart as a natural consequence of sleep deprivation, restricted diets, weak command structure, and a complete lack of formal training in sustaining a long-term siege against superior numbers. Also working against the warriors was the fact that they were never a cohesive group and had considerable mistrust among their ranks. Then there was the substance abuse problem. At Akwesasne the warriors were free and open in their use of drugs and alcohol, habits they brought to Kanehsatake, yet never curtailed. Those more extreme in their abuse were told to leave, but to remove all mind-altering substances would have decimated the warriors almost to a man.

By late September, those warriors at the treatment center had come to the bitter realization that they had nothing left to fight with. The leaders of Kanehsatake wanted them out, while many of the key Kahnawake-based warriors, those who had accelerated the crisis by blocking the Mercier Bridge, had fled the province, fearing arrest. The attack teams involved in the Akwesasne battle were more concerned with getting the casinos up and going while resuming their highly lucrative smuggling operations. Kanehsatake was becoming bad for business. On September 26 they burned their weapons, left the treatment center, and were promptly arrested by the Canadian authorities, who levied fairly minor charges against them given the potential for the massive loss of human life in both Mohawk communities.

While some may say in their defense that this small band was defending the aboriginal rights of the Mohawk Nation, virtually all their actions were taken without the knowledge or consent of the Mohawk people. The warriors rejected the Haudenosaunee Confederacy as a legitimate entity and defied the Mohawk Nation Council. Any entity, or individual, who challenged their actions or threatened their various criminal enterprises was placed at risk and labeled as a traitor, deserving forcible eviction or outright execution. They could not have sustained their posturing without the compliance of the media, who brushed aside all credibility standards in order to fit preconceived agendas. The truth was an inconvenience for inept, adrenaline junkie reporters who completely failed to connect the killers of Akwesasne with the "freedom fighters" at Oka. And by doing so, the media insured that those warrior leaders who gave the "shoot to kill" orders that took the lives of Harold Edwards and Mathew Pyke would escape liability for capital crimes which have haunted the Mohawk people for the past generation.

From being a quiet, secluded, and stable community for most of its history, Kanehsatake was thrust into chaos when the factions caused by the events of 1990 vied for control over the territory. Without a stable, centralized government with effective law enforcement powers, there was no way to control the more extreme elements who used warrior intimidation tactics to create a climate of fear and intimidation. The resulting anarchy meant Kanehsatake became a haven for warriors who served the drug trade as traffickers, distributing cocaine and marijuana to dealers in the Montreal area, or who profited from the harvests of their own hydroponics farms. While the Mohawk police agency on the reserve knew who the dealers were, they certainly did not go to any great lengths to hide because the political in-fighting prevented the police from doing their job and arresting the dope peddlers. When any external police agency entered Kanehsatake, they were confronted by masked men waving the blood red death's head banner of the warrior society that had become quite popular across Canada whenever aboriginal people elected to challenge the state.

The disintegration of Kanehsatake was complete by 2004. The elected band council collapsed amid plans by the council's chief to investigate and prosecute the drug dealers. Some viewed the actions of Chief James Gabriel as treasonous since they would have meant cooperating with the despised Surete du Quebec, while others wanted control over their community wrestled back from the traffickers, even if that meant long jail terms in a Quebec prison. In the spring of 2004 Gabriel was driven from his Kanehsatake home, which was then set on fire. The chief of the Kanehsatake Mohawk Police was fired, but his replacements were no more effective in restoring order to the community. Their patrol cars were smashed and their headquarters surrounded by the opponents of Gabriel. Though the various acts of violence were videotaped, the provincial authorities were extremely reluctant to arrest the suspects, who grew bolder in their demands for Gabriel to resign; a destructive spring turned into an unsettled summer. Without the traditional Mohawk reconciliation and healing rituals, Kanehsatake never had a chance to recover from 1990. That summer's bitterness is now being carried on to the next generation and beyond, resulting in a legacy not of bold freedom fighters taking on the world, but of parasites eager to consume the flesh of what is left of Mohawk nationalism.

CHAPTER 12

❧

Out of the Ashes

The Mohawks barely endured the civil discord caused by infighting, but the curse of factionalism plagued other Iroquois nations as well. Some elected to go their own way, disregarding the Confederacy and embracing the new economic development opportunities offered by commercial gambling. The land claims initiatives followed suit with the nations pursuing their own strategies without consultation with the other Iroquois. The end result was the absence of a common stance on the most important issue in many generations.

The unity of the Haudenosaunee was shattered on the land claims issue. The nations were picked apart by New York State and left vulnerable when they took their claims into a court system that was becoming increasingly hostile to Native issues in general. The legal defeats suffered by the Oneida Nation of New York (ONNY) and the Cayugas in the spring of 2005 dealt a suspected and fatal blow to Iroquois land claims. The Oneida case, in particular, was galling to the other Iroquois nations since it involved a dispute over $8,000 in land taxes the city of Sherrill claimed was owed to it by the ONNY.

After years of untempered arrogance the Oneida leadership refused to work out a deal with Sherrill and initiated legal action which, it believed, would enhance its status as a Native nation by having the U.S. federal courts affirm its exemption from state and county taxes.

Meanwhile, the Oneida leadership continued its attacks on its relatives from Wisconsin and Ontario. In 1995, several dozen Oneidas had all of their membership benefits suspended by the men's council of ONNY because, the council said, they had committed treasonous acts by meeting with their kin from the west.

Thereafter, any New York–based Oneidas lived in apprehension of being seen in public with their relatives. Whatever chance there was for the Oneida people to discuss collective issues, such as land claims and culture, was dashed by ONNY, a decision that greatly weakened the Oneida bargaining position with New York State and undermined its legal case.

ONNY officials blasted their kinfolk as sellouts who had abandoned their ancestral homes, an accusation which was not relegated to events that had occurred 170 years in the past, but was made as if contemporary Oneidas in Wisconsin and Ontario were the guilty parties. In a disturbing contradiction that the regional media elected to ignore, the top two positions on the men's council of ONNY were held by individuals whose only claim to Oneida status came from their immediate ancestors in Southwold, Ontario.

The one Oneida group that had stayed in the area was the Marble Hill Oneidas, who had a small community south of the city of Sherrill and had been, for the most part, ignored by ONNY until it began to apply for federal aid.

Armed with an expensive company of lawyers, ONNY was used to getting its way in Madison and Oneida counties and purchased thousands of acres of land in the contested areas and refused to pay land taxes. Dozens of homes on these newly acquired sections were bulldozed rather than dispersed to Oneida families in desperate need of housing. Individuals working for ONNY were warned not to speak to the press, and oaths of confidentiality were required prior to employment. There was no recourse for those who were fired since ONNY has sovereign immunity from individual lawsuits.

Arrogant, prosperous, and rude, ONNY had every reason to expect its case against Sherrill would go its way. But it had not taken an accurate survey of the U.S. Supreme Court, nor had it made adequate analysis of the Court's recent decisions regarding aboriginal issues, many of which went against the notion that an Indian nation had an unfettered right to claim sovereignty over whatever piece of land it chose to buy.

At some point the Indian nations were going to have to pay a share of the costs for roads, schools, and utilities, public services which were expensive and tough to bear by the average taxpayer. ONNY did not understand this, so when the spring ruling of 2005 was handed down in favor of Sherrill, the shock was so intense that it silenced its public relations bureau for many days.

The opponents of ONNY, and of Indian sovereignty in general, were ecstatic. They knew the Court's decision had changed the political/legal climate in New

York State and across the country. Indian governments would now most likely pay billions in taxes on newly acquired lands, and they would have to pay billions more on the businesses that operated on those lands.

Oddly, no national or regional Native organization saw the Supreme Court's decision as sufficient cause for alarm. No statements were made condemning the Court or ONNY for placing Native rights in jeopardy. Instead, the leadership of ONNY went on to verbally attack Governor Pataki and other Oneidas in statements on television and in newspapers. In July 2005, at a hearing before the committee of the U.S. House of Representatives, an ONNY official did not spend his time calling for unity in light of the legal setback, but instead viciously attacked the Wisconsin Oneidas for tendering a land claims settlement package to New York State without consulting, or securing the approval of, the ONNY.

On June 28 the Iroquois suffered another blow to their hopes of extending their land holdings when the U.S. Second Circuit Court of Appeals dismissed the land claims of the Cayuga Nation and reversed a $248 million judgment it had won before a trial judge. The Second Circuit judges ruled that the Cayugas had waited too long to bring their case and that if their claim was sustained, it would disrupt the lives of thousands of residents within the contested area. The Cayuga case was certainly not helped by serious in-fighting as to who were its true leaders.

The Cayuga case sent shock waves throughout the Iroquois Confederacy. Where previously, the nations had a strong negotiating stance with New York State officials, they were now effectively toothless. The casinos-for-land faction was seen as the culprit for they had split the Confederacy apart in their drive to secure gambling revenues, even when repeatedly warned that such tactics would destroy the very sovereignty commercial gambling must, of necessity, exploit.

In the late winter of 2005 New York Governor George Pataki had proposed five casinos in the Catskills resort area northwest of New York City, a plan which was meant to terminate the land claims of the Wisconsin Oneidas, the Stockbridge-Munsees of Wisconsin, the Cayugas of New York, the Seneca-Cayugas of Oklahoma, and the St. Regis Mohawks of Akwesasne. By spring, he had scaled back his plans to include only a couple casinos, but armed with favorable court rulings, he was in a position to pick and choose which Native factions would be awarded a casino deal.

New York's constitution prohibits casino-style gambling, but it was uncertain if the document applied to Indian reservations. After the U.S. Supreme

Court ruling in March 2005 it was clear that no Native nation could claim exemption from state regulations outside those boundaries that had been previously acknowledged as Indian country by the Bureau of Indian Affairs. Pataki could lobby to have land in the Catskills designated as such, which would then enable a casino to be built, but a long and intense legal battle from anticasino forces may well scuttle that plan.

Among the Mohawks, internal opposition to the November 2004 land claims deal continued to grow. The St. Regis Tribal Council had rammed through a referendum to endorse the settlement package, which included, among other things, reduced electrical rates for the reservation, a $100 million payment by New York spaced over several years, the option to buy up to 13,000 acres of land adjacent to the reservation, and free tuition for Mohawk students at the State University of New York campuses.

No mention was made of preserving the tax-free status of the Mohawks, nor was the sticky question of jurisdiction resolved. The Mohawk Nation Council of Chiefs and the Canadian-based Mohawk Council of Akwesasne were involved in the presettlement negotiations, yet it was unclear what benefits, if any, they would receive from the deal.

The longhouse people, as represented by the Mohawk Nation Council, held a series of clan meetings about the settlement but failed to arrive at a consensus as to whether they should support or reject the proposal. Considerable anger resulted when a member of the Council unilaterally elected to join the other two Mohawk agencies and sign the settlement at a discreet location 60 miles away from Akwesasne.

It became obvious in the following weeks that the longhouse people were made to believe that if they did not agree, they would receive nothing, yet they had come to realize that all the tangible benefits coming from the settlement would be channeled through the St. Regis Tribal Council.

The controversy empowered another faction at Akwesasne, which called itself the Kaiienkehaka Nation. A breakaway group from the longhouse, its leadership promised direct action if the settlement was approved. They argued the deal did nothing to protect the independent status of the Mohawks and was in breach of the Two Row Wampum, a treaty entered into with Holland in the 1620s and said to be binding on the United States.

The Two Row Wampum pledges its parties to refrain from applying its laws to one another and that the Iroquois shall always have the right to self-determination. It used the imagery of the Europeans in their sailing ships and the Iroquois in their canoes floating upon a fast-moving stream. Just as it would be dangerous to attempt to cross from the canoe to the ship, so too would it be risky to try to effect jurisdiction over another nation.

The Kaiienkehaka Nation made an effective presentation before a committee of the New York State Assembly in April 2005, which put a bit of a brake on the State's endorsement of the November settlement. But in July St. Regis Tribal officials went to Washington to appeal to the U.S. House of Representatives to endorse the settlement as agreed.

There was anger not only at Akwesasne but among the other Mohawk communities, none of which had been consulted during the settlement negotiations. The Mohawk Council of Kahnawake attempted to launch a legal challenge in the U.S. courts but was quickly rebuffed. Nor was the Grand Council of the Haudenosaunee Confederacy asked to review the settlement's provisions, a remarkable omission given its implications for the Onondagas and Senecas.

The Onondaga Nation made a formal claim to thousands of acres (including most of what is now Syracuse University) when it submitted its land actions in the U.S. courts in March 2005 just two weeks before the Oneidas suffered their historic defeat. The Onondaga approach was significantly different than the Oneidas. Whereas the Oneida Nation of New York was belligerent, aggressive, and arrogant, the Onondagas adopted a strategy aimed at winning the support of those residents who lived on what was once reservation land. They made repeated assurances that no one would be ejected from his home and laced this with a strong appeal for the ecological restoration of the region. The Onondagas also used various public forums, including the media, to explain the basis of their claims as well as their commitment to being good neighbors. They stated that under no circumstances would they barter away their lands for casinos, unlike their Iroquois kin.

In July 2005 the Onondagas amended their claims in anticipation that New York, as the principal defendant, would make reference to the Cayuga case. Called "laches," this argument holds that if a plaintiff waits an unreasonable time before bringing action for redress, their claim is void. The Onondagas had ample proof to show that there had been an ongoing effort to secure lost lands, but the U.S. courts are unlikely to overturn the Oneida and Cayuga decisions.

In retrospect, the Iroquois have repeated the mistakes their ancestors made during and after the American Revolution. They allowed external interests to break them apart, thereby weakening their legal and political status. The Grand Council made decisions meant to remove internal threats, but without decisive enforcement action, those pronouncements carried little real meaning to most Iroquois people.

Just as in 1777, the Oneidas, as the weakest link, were able to be broken into hostile factions by New York State and the U.S. federal government. The Grand Council made a decision in May 1993 that the Oneida leadership was illegitimate under Iroquois law and must be replaced with a traditional council consisting of chiefs and clanmothers. But the Oneida people were not given the physical support they needed to restore such a council, hence dismissal of the Grand Council's authority by Arthur Raymond Halbritter, the self-proclaimed representative of the ONNY. Halbritter was able to secure the support of U.S. Congressman Sherwood Boehlert, a moderate Republican who reportedly persuaded the Clinton administration to ignore the Grand Council and order the Bureau of Indian Affairs to reinstate the Oneida representative.

Again, no action was taken to support the restoration of a traditional government for the Oneidas, an entity which would, had it existed, been bound under Iroquois law to adhere to an antigambling agenda. Emboldened by the positivity of the other Iroquois, the ONNY accelerated its gambling ventures and created its own courts (none of its judges are Native), which followed laws and procedures based on New York State statutes. It specifically asked permission from the legislature to empower the Oneida Nation Police (again, no Natives actually work as cops) to enforce State laws on Indian territory.

The Oneida Nation entered into secretive contracts, gave money to political candidates, urged its members to vote in U.S. and regional elections, ceded jurisdiction over parts of its casino operations to New York, paid U.S. and State taxes, and generally picked and chose when and where it would claim exemptions based on Indian sovereignty.

All of these potentially lethal compromises were ignored by the other Iroquois. And just as in that terrible time after the Revolution, the Oneidas, despite their claims to be the most loyal of U.S. allies, were once again the first Iroquois nation to be stripped of their ancestral rights. Despite the ready access to books, original documents, and historians, the Iroquois followed the same destructive paths of their ancestors. Their many lawyers, arrogant and profit minded, either would not or could not advise their clients to stand together on issues of mutual concern.

The number of American law enforcement agents guarding the country against illegal entry was greatly increased after the collapse of the World Trade Center on September 11, 2001.

Mohawks had worked raising the towers and were among the first on the scene after the collapse. Their ironworking skills of cutting metal and moving steel were put to effective use in the following months as the Twin Towers site was cleared.

The ironworkers returned home to Akwesasne to find a community that had come under intense scrutiny by the American government. The newly formed Department of Homeland Security was concerned about the flow of illegal aliens through Akwesasne, a highly profitable activity which was substantially curtailed after the attack on the World Trade Center.

Akwesasne had been identified as an open conduit for smuggled humans, tobacco, and narcotics. Such activities would be impossible for the Mohawks to sustain without connections with organized crime involvement. Southeast Asians were brought to the reservation by Toronto-based Chinese tongs, while other gangs provided narcotics. Both were designated for transport into the United States, but the tobacco was Canada bound.

The increased police presence on or near the reservation resulted in more smuggling arrests, but during any given night, high-speed boats loaded with contraband, their bow lights turned off, can be heard slashing across the St. Lawrence River.

In contrast, since 1990, the Canadian federal and provincial governments have poured tens of millions of dollars into Akwesasne, enabling the community to oversee the building of a medical center, arena, elders' residences, and dozens of new homes. Funds were given by the Canadians to support Mohawk culture, enabling the reservation schools to offer instruction in the Mohawk language. Money was also given to develop alternative healing methods and substance abuse programs, along with youth and women's shelters. Still more money was spent on postsecondary school grants, environmental studies, and resource conservation initiatives.

Mohawk-owned businesses secured government-backed loans and grants, resulting in the building of a small strip mall and enterprises ranging from lacrosse stick manufacturing to large-scale construction companies. This curious mixture of legitimate and illicit economies brought unparalleled material wealth to the Mohawks, but it was not without conflict.

By far, the most lucrative money-generating activity was drug smuggling. The risks of carrying narcotics had risen since 2001, but the rewards were substantial. Teenagers were actively solicited by the smuggling cartels since they were told it was unlikely they would be imprisoned if they were caught. A few hours on a boat netted them more money than their parents earned in a month, or so went the rationale.

Inevitably, violence in the form of assaults, hijacking, and murders became intertwined with the drug smuggling and the too easy prosperity. Since the community was divided into competing political factions, there was no chance of internally curtailing the smuggling or investigating the full extent of the various criminal enterprises that were tearing at the Mohawk soul. Many Akwesasne residents believed that only a military occupation by joint U.S.–Canadian armed forces could stop the trafficking.

Despite these challenges and distractions, the Mohawks continued to adhere to a collective identity defined by family, the bonds of a common ancestry, and the desire, however vague or muted, to preserve a distinct aboriginal heritage. On the surface the Mohawks seemed to have become overwhelmed and obscured by a consumer culture, yet every lunar month, the traditional faction gathered at the communal longhouse to carry on the most ancient of Iroquois rituals. Spoken exclusively in Mohawk, the ceremonies are meant to direct the attention of human beings toward the natural world, then engage in a series of prayers, dances, and songs meant to express their gratitude for the infinite blessings of life.

The "thanksgiving address," called, in Mohawk, Ohenten Kariwatekwen, begins each ceremony when a male clan leader, either a chief or faith-keeper, holds long strands of sacred wampum, then speaks to the earth's waters, lands, plants, insects, fish, animals, trees, winds, birds, thunder, and medicines, each of which is told of the gratitude the Mohawks have for their being.

Sun, moon, and stars (along with four spiritual beings) who watch humans from the horizons of the earth, are also thanked for their contentment to fulfill their instructions as given to them by the Creator. Special mention is accorded to the Seneca prophet Skaniiateriio (c. 1734–1815), or Handsome Lake, a visionary who provided the Iroquois with a set of moral codes by which they were to survive European contact. The speaker concludes by addressing Sonkwiatison, the Creator, a mysterious benevolent force who presented the Mohawks with everything they required to live in peace and harmony in one of the most fertile and beautiful places on earth.

The address is followed by speeches, in which the people are told of the reason for the gathering, be it to honor the berry plants (the Strawberry Ceremony) or to express their gratitude for successfully growing crops (Harvest). Sacred songs and dances encourage the participation of everyone in attendance. Virtually every Mohawk ritual is characterized by the music produced from voice, small drums, and horn rattles.

While only a small faction of the Mohawk people actually attend the long-house ceremonies, the nation as a whole derives its essence from the ability to point to them as clear evidence of the viability, strength, and integrity of Mohawk culture.

Since 1979, the Mohawk Nation has taken a decisive step toward insuring the survival of its heritage by sponsoring the Akwesasne Freedom School, an institution which provides complete immersion in the Mohawk language in an academic setting from kindergarten to grade eight. The school's highly creative curriculum is structured in a way to provide a strong background in science, grammar, the social sciences, and Mohawk culture, and though only a small percentage of reservation parents have elected to send their children there, it, as does the longhouse, contributes greatly to the communal dynamic that has enabled the Mohawks to maintain more of their Native identity than any other aboriginal nation east of the Mississippi.

Since 1990, there has been an enormous output in books, music, fine arts, and crafts from the Iroquois people. The People Building the Longhouse have moved aggressively into film, acting, radio broadcasting, and creative writing. At no time in the past seven generations have the Iroquois been as creative as they are at the dawn of the twenty-first century.

Despite the loss of language and the traditional lifestyle, the Iroquois cling with incredible determination to what they have left. Those who adhere to the traditional principles have embraced the prophecies that are an important part of the Handsome Lake teachings. They are confident the prophecies are unambiguous markers of the events, both regional and planetary, which will not only bring about a resurgence of Iroquois power, but will stop the mad dash toward ecological suicide.

Traditional leaders of the previous and current generations have spoken at forums throughout the world in protest of the destruction of the planet, marked by the muting of those indigenous peoples whose lives depend on maintaining a delicate, easily tipped balance between nature and its most aggressive offspring. The late Leon Shenandoah, Tadodaho of the Haudenosaunee before his passing in 1996, gave harsh warning to the world's nations if they silenced native peoples. Those who lived in the land were of the land; they spoke nature's language and moved to her rhythms. Displace them, silence them, integrate and convert them at great risk to us all.

Shenandoah was blunt but never without compassion. He spoke of a time when the pure waters of the Haudenosaunee would be unfit to drink, the fish inedible, the sacred elm and maple trees infected with diseases before they disappeared from our lands. He said it was foretold of how we would lose our languages and become insane with alcohol. We would observe strange, incurable diseases, the extinction of many animals, and a time of great confusion when the Haudenosaunee would, as they did in 1777, come to blows as we fought each other. We would be seduced by a powerful, material culture which would reduce the traditional people to but a small fraction of the entire Iroquois people.

But, Shenandoah cautioned, this time of change would affect everyone on the earth. Great winds would come about to sweep the land, droughts would diminish our crops, and the thunder beings, those guardians of the sky, would become so angry with the behavior of the humans that they would refuse to bring their life-giving rains from the west.

Even the strawberry, that most sacred of foods, would withhold its fruit until we were left with nothing but its delicate leaves. Then the Great White Pine, the everlasting Haudenosaunee, would tremble and fall, its roots ripping up the soil as it screeched toward the ground. Should it strike the earth, all would be lost, but, it is believed, the traditional leaders will step forward, interlock their arms, and stop the tree's fall. They will join beneath its tremendous trunk to push it back until its roots are once again placed into the soil and its peak touches the heavens, to connect sky and earth.

Silver and Gold

©J. Shenandoah

They brought back two serpents
One Silver, one Gold
They were shiny and bright
a delight to behold

Proud of themselves
and enjoying the glow
Feeding the serpents
and the evil began to grow

People fought amongst themselves
on nothing they could agree
and the serpent began devouring
every living being

They left a trail . . . of destruction
Cut through mountains, rivers, and streams
They marred the earth as they devoured
our children's and ancestors' dreams

To the north and . . . the south
they destroyed all in their path
They all feared the serpents
and they wondered, Would they last?

They left a trail . . . of destruction
Cut through mountains, rivers, and streams
They marred the earth as they devoured
our children's and ancestors' dreams

One day we spotted . . . something in the distance
Oh yes . . . it sparkled of silver and gold
We remembered a story . . . of near destruction
a time when serpents ruled . . . the world

So we called to the boy whose arrow
would save us from this ruin
With a white flint arrow and clanmother's hair
with a bow from the willow—the people will be spared

Our people will be spared
With a white flint arrow and strand of hair
with a bow from the willow—our people will be spared
Our people will be spared

Appendix
∽

Statement of Doug George-Kanentiio
May 15, 1990
Valleyfield De Salleberry Jail

On Sunday morning, May 13, 1990, I was sleeping at the North American Indian Travelling College on Cornwall Island, Akwesasne. I had been staying at the College to assist in media relations, help with security and any other task that needed completing. At 7:45 A.M. I was awakened by Brian David, a resident of St. Regis Village. He informed me that my brother, David George Jr., had been arrested by the Surete du Quebec a short time before and was being charged with accomplice in a murder. Once we began calling over the College telephones to find out more information we heard Ernest King, Steve Lazore and Roger Mitchell, all of the Akwesasne Police, had been taken, along with my brother, to Montreal by helicopter. We also learned Snye resident Kenneth Lazore was also taken to Montreal for questioning in the killing of Harold "Junior" Edwards.

An attorney, Paul Williams, was at the College throughout the day attempting to obtain information from the Surete about the five men but had a difficult time with the police. He called attorney Phillip Schneider in Montreal to make sure the men were given access to counsel. Throughout the day we tried to make contact with the men in Montreal as well as inform others we thought might be arrested to insure they were aware of the situation and to assure them we were ready to assist in the protection of their rights.

As the day progressed it was clear to me the Surete Quebec had selected the men who were at my brother's residence on May 1 as subjects of investigation and possible arrest for at least one of the killings, most probably that of Harold Edwards. I knew their perceptions (the Surete) were wrong. After it became apparent the men held in Montreal were not going to be released I felt that since I was also in Snye on May 1 my recollections might be of help to them.

In the early afternoon I was told by Paul Williams to remain at the College since he had been told by the Surete I was also a suspect. They had informed him a rifle used at the scene by at least two of us had been determined to have fired the bullet which killed Edwards. I tried hard to remember the exact details of that day, May 1, and to recall what I had said to two investigators from Quebec in a statement I had signed on May 2.

Late that afternoon, Paul Williams said they wanted to question me in Snye at a temporary Surete station. I knew this "questioning" might turn into an arrest so I prepared myself accordingly by dressing simply. I was taken to Snye by a Quebec investigator in the company of Paul Williams and Mohawk Council of Akwesasne chief Lloyd Benedict. I thought while being driven to Snye that if the helicopter was not there I would not be arrested and possibly my brother, along with the others, would be released.

Once in Snye, we were told by the investigators they wanted additional information, mainly as to whether or nor I had used a 30–06 during the May 1 fight. I said I could only remember passing such a rifle from Ken Lazore from a basement window up to a porch at my brother's home. The helicopter arrived during the interrogation so I knew I was to be arrested. I went willingly because I had nothing to hide and had spoke only the truth. The investigators tried to convince me they had statements from Roger Mitchell and Ken Lazore which indicated I had admitted to killing Edwards. They gave hints of this before the helicopter transfer to Montreal but emphasized this while they were interrogating me there. I was told by Paul Williams that I should not take a polygraph test on the advice of attorney Schneider but, again, I believed I could answer truthfully as to my actions of May 1 and could respond negatively to any accusation as to the alleged killing of Junior Edwards.

In Montreal, I was first questioned by the same two investigators I had made the May 2 statement to. I was then taken to the polygraph testing room and locked in. The polygraph investigator was initially friendly as he attempted to gain my trust. I realized his actions were a charade, an act, and a professional response. Nonetheless I answered his questions truthfully. He asked about my family, whom I trusted, my job, my income. He made many notations in his clipboard. He went so far as to make use of my mother's death (in 1965) in his psychological survey. He said Ken Lazore had passed the test and that I was implicated in the murder.

After hooking me up to the machine, he gave me a test using flash cards and numbers. He said I responded well to the test. He explained the mechanics of the machine to me although I had read the pamphlet he had given to me. He asked a series of mundane questions about my identity. I realized that if I "failed" the police would turn their attention on me full force. Despite their earlier assurances, in Snye, to Paul Williams that I'd be released pending the outcome of the polygraph I knew that was not to be the case. I recall clearly my reactions to the question "Did you kill Junior Edwards?" At the word "kill" I felt shock but my responses in all three series of questions was "no." After the detective left, again locking the door, I felt apprehension and wariness but relief I had spoken the absolute truth. There was no doubt in my mind I did not kill Junior Edwards.

When the detective returned, his manner was completely changed. He was belligerent, hostile, and accusatory. He said many times that the test showed I had killed Edwards. He showed me the Graph which I signed. I attempted to show him that since the questions had come in 12-second intervals I reacted only to the word "kill" and that when I said "no" the graph was flat. He would not tolerate my questions but attempted to gain an emotional reaction by appealing to my compassion for the Edwards family. He made a number of sarcastic remarks about my "cause," how I was "dragging down the others with me" and that in conclusion I was "not worth the sweat off his balls."

I was then taken to another floor and given the same abusive treatment by the initial detectives. They said I would be charged with 1st degree murder. They flashed a statement allegedly signed by Roger Mitchell which supposedly implicated me. They said Ken Lazore had told them I used the 30–06, went to the house where Edwards was shot and later was seen running down the road before telling Officer Mitchell and Ken Lazore I had shot someone. They said I was being watched by at least one person with binoculars from St. Regis Village and that a television crew had filmed the entire event. They also asserted that I staged the event for publicity purposes, that we had fired indiscriminately, that the "warriors" were not involved.

I attempted to ask about the Mathew Pyke investigation but they did not respond. They were abusive, loud and gave the appearance of being angry. I did not make any admission or statements other than I was tired and wanted to speak with Paul Williams, my attorney. They finally allowed Paul to talk to me. I told him they had accused me of murder and that I, according to them, failed the polygraph. I was then told by Paul what to expect that night. I had been informed of my rights by the police.

I was taken to a holding cell for the night. Roger Mitchell was going through the process of formal arrest just as I was leaving the search area. I was told I would not see my brother although he was near. Throughout the night, I tried to remember what exactly happened on May 1. I firmly believed no one at my brother's that day killed Edwards. I felt they were looking for a scapegoat because of the intense pressure upon the police to make an arrest by the politicians and the press.

There were blanks in my recollections but I was absolutely sure I did not walk along the shore, stalk Edwards and kill him. That charge was ridiculous. About 1:00 P.M. I was taken from the cell. Steve Lazore was in the one next to mine. I signaled to him I was okay and tried to tell him I was being charged with murder. I was fingerprinted and asked if I had an arrest warrant in Sarnia, Ontario which I did not. I was driven by two detectives, handcuffed, to the Surete Quebec station in Valleyfield. For two and a half hours, I was in a holding cell with my brother Davey and Ken Lazore. We felt we were being subject to electronic surveillance. Nonetheless, we talked freely for we had nothing to hide. Ken told me of how they had used exactly the same abusive tactics on him, even down to the accusation he had "failed" the polygraph and the "sweat on his balls" remark.

Davey said he had been hit by one of them but refused to talk on his lawyer's advice despite 6 hours of interrogation. The police were obviously trying to get us to implicate each other. They lied about supposed "statements" and mysterious "witnesses." They said they had absolute ballistic proof the bullet which killed Edwards came from a 30–06 I had shot. We doubted they had such evidence given their attempts to force us to admit to our "guilt." We expressed agreement as to how easily they abused us as people, as Indians. We felt the same about one thing: the arrests were more press-oriented than factual. We noticed three Akwesasne Police officers arrive at the station and recognized Lewis Mitchell and Sonny Caldwell.

Around 5 P.M. the detectives handcuffed Davey and myself together. We asked if there was a less public way of entering the Valleyfield jail since we were told over 200 media people were there. Nonetheless they drove us, using two marked police cruises in front and back, to the jail. It was a massive publicity stunt. We were pushed and dragged through the TV crews, the reporters. Many people were shoved out of the way.

When we arrived in court I noticed many Akwesasne people there including my family. We were told of the charges against us. I was very glad my brother was to be released; I knew Ken, Roger and Steve would also be set free. I was told the charge against me was 2nd degree murder. I felt it was only because I had been visible in my remarks to the press about the terrorist warriors and the investigation in general.

I was taken to the Valleyfield jail where I am presently confined.

May 15/1990
Statement of May 15/1990 Regarding April 30–May 1
Gun Battle at the Akwesasne Mohawk Territory

Present at the residence of David George, Jr., River Road, Snye District, Akwesasne Mohawk Reserve April 30–May 1:

David "Davey" George Jr., Doug George, Ron Lazore, Larry "Cochise" David, Joseph Lazore, Kevin King, Brian David, Richard "Cartoon" Alfred-Tronnekwe, Dave Francis, Harvey Arquette, Ken Lazore plus Eric Seibling and Ryan Ramirez of the *Canadian Press.*

Early in the evening of April 30 a group of Akwesasne men were asked if they wanted to go to Snye to defend the last area (other than Cornwall Island) not overrun by the Mohawk Sovereignty Security Force (the "warriors") and the pro-gamblers. Since April 27 my brother had, with my help and four others (Dean George, Cartoon, Perry Thompson, Tony Lafrance Jr.) defended his home against repeated attacks by snipers. Two newsmen, Eric Seibling and the photographer Ramirez, wanted to be there. We left the North American Traveling College on Cornwall Island. Dave Francis, Kevin King, Ron Lazore and myself drove to my brother's residence. We got there at dusk. A number of firearms were already in the immediate area including shotguns, hunting rifles, an AKS assault rifle (semi-automatic) and two AR 15 rifles (also semi-automatic) of .223 caliber. There was a single shot .222 bolt action rifle (but with no bullets) and three 30–06 hunting rifles.

Between 10 and 11 P.M. I, along with Ron Lazore, Harvey Arquette, Larry David, Joe Lazore, possibly Ken Lazore, were on the river banks on the north part of my brother's property. A boat left near the Lincoln Roundpoint home in St. Regis. We knew there were snipers intending to shoot us on St. Regis Island and Yellow Island. One sniper group was reportedly at the Roundpoint smuggling complex on the western edge of St. Regis Island and another at a point across the river from my brother's.

The boat reached a point across from us in the middle of the St. Regis River. Shots were fired at us from the hill behind my brother's home. I did not shoot. Shortly before I had been given an AR 15 rifle with four clips and 3 boxes of extra ammunition (20 rounds per box). Although better armed than in the previous three days we did not expect to be attacked by sustained gunfire. From that initial exchange of gunfire until 1:30 A.M. it was relatively quiet. I remained at the river shore about 40 feet from a dock, west of a woodpile and at all times in contact with Ron Lazore, Joe Lazore or Brian David. For warmth, I used a light colored blanket. At the time of the second attack I was almost asleep.

While I was at the shore we were fired upon with hundreds of rounds coming from the hill and from an area near the Jacobs' and Lazore residence on River Road west of my brother's. I heard many bullets pass over my head and at that time returned fire but did so without seeing anyone. I emptied one clip in the general area of the west but could not see either the Jacobs or Lazore homes.

After the initial attack, I left the shoreline to see what had happened and to check and make sure everyone was okay. Assured no one had been hit I went to a position in front of my brother's, along the road, east of his house and behind a stone fence. Behind me, at a distance of 20 feet, was Kevin King. To my right, behind a flower box, was Dave Francis. On his right was Harvey Arquette and on his right were Brian David and Cochise David. Tronnekwe was in the house at times. Ron Lazore was moving about, taking charge. Joe Lazore was in the area as was my brother. Ken Lazore remained in the basement of my brother's house as were the reporters. We had a scanner hooked up outside.

Throughout the night the attackers, we assumed they were Mohawk Sovereignty Security Force, kept up a taunting, abusive series of verbal attacks over the scanner. We recognized the voices of Matthew Herne, Diane Lazore, Gordon Lazore, Pat Thomas. They said many times over the scanner they were going to kill us. This was recorded by Eddie Gray at his home on Cook Road.

The exchange of gunfire was very intense at times. We were greatly outgunned, and towards daybreak, running low on ammunition. I, along with the others, fired periodically, in controlled bursts, under the direction of Ron Lazore or Tronnekwe.

At about 4:30 or 5 A.M. we heard rapid gunfire directed to the east of us by the assailants on the hill. A group of men, 14 in number, were coming to assist us. They were shot at by people on the hill and also assailants in a small woods on the Paul King property. For some time most of the gunfire by those on the hill was directed there. I left my position when it was fully light to take a position at the northern corner of my brother's house under a porch with a view of the western slope of the hill from where the shooting was coming from. I fired a few rounds towards the hill and heard many bullets pass over the house.

At one time, Ken Lazore opened a basement window. I asked if the reporters were okay. He passed a 30–06 rifle to me but since I had the AR 15 I could not use the rifle. I put it, or passed it, up to the porch because we needed a rifle with a scope to see who had been firing at us from St. Regis Village. I went to follow Joe Lazore to the home of Lewis Mitchell. At the corner of the Mitchell home Joe periodically checked the Gordon Lazore house because we were being constantly fired at from there. There was heavy gunfire directed at our relief team to the east of us. We saw one of our vehicles parked next to a backhoe in the road but could not see our men. The photographer then joined us for a cigarette. I cautioned him against getting shot and told him how to crawl up the hill. While the sun was rising I went back to my brother's yard. I met Ken Lazore next to the river, behind my brother's fishing equipment shed. There I used his 30–06 (I don't know how it got there) to fire two rounds towards the hill from where the shots were coming from. Ken also fired a number of rounds. Using the scope I saw nothing, or anyone, unusual. The targets we had were the middle parts of trees on the hill.

Afterwards, I went to the stone wall near the road to the west of my brother's home. There were rifles including a 30–30 Winchester. I fired a few rounds but again saw nothing to shoot at. Still in possession of the AR 15 I fired a few more rounds towards the hill. At one time Tronnekwe went up the hill to investigate. He came back and a group of us charged the hill. Cochise, Harvey Arquette, myself, Tronnekwe, Dave Francis took the hill. The attackers had abandoned their points. We received no more gunfire after that. My brother and Brian David joined us as they came from the west part of the hill. With help from our relief people, including Steve Barnes and Mike White, we went east to clear out the Gordon Lazore house of snipers. Having done so we then went back to my brother's. I went down to the river with Brian David. Ken Lazore was working on the Akwesasne Police boat to get it ready in case we needed it.

I heard yelling towards the front of the house and when I went to investigate I was told a man was waving a white shirt to the west of us near the fallen tree on River Road. I saw a man with his hands up. One of our relief men,

Dave King, went with Dave Francis to bring the man to us. I went up to the Basil Thompson house but stopped along the northern edge of the road. I had the AR 15. At one time I stepped off the road onto a metal stair to protect our men in case they were shot at. I then walked with them (Dave Francis and Dave King) to escort the surrendering man, Arthur Yopps, to the flower box in front of my brother's.

We asked Yopps a number of questions after he gave us his license. I asked him specifically where he obtained his weapon, a modified Ruger Mini 14 .223 caliber; he said from a man whose name started with a "B." I asked him who was shooting at us, he said he did not recognize most of them. I asked if anyone was hurt for we had heard them call for assistance earlier. He said one man had been hit, grazed by a bullet in the upper right arm. He said that was all the injuries he knew of. Dave Francis fired one round from the Mini 14; it was later given to Roger Mitchell of the Akwesasne Police. After asking Yopps my questions I went to sit on the riverbank with Brian David. Yopps wanted to talk to my brother about a cease-fire.

Shortly afterwards I heard yelling and saw Yopps running west on River Road. I was told Gordon Lazore also showed up but went back into the brush on the hill. From that time until I left the area at 4 P.M. I gave interviews with the press and stayed in close contact with all the men. We learned of Mathew Pyke's death that afternoon. At 4 P.M. a reporter, Joseph Gray, told my brother Dean there was someone lying at the Raymond Lazore house. I did not learn until later it was Junior Edwards. Dave Francis, my brother Dean and myself left the area after failing to find Davey. David Francis fired four shots into the air and then we left.

May 16, 1990

Bibliography

Benn, Carl. *The Iroquois in the War of 1812*. Toronto: Univ. of Toronto Press, 1998.

Deloria, Vine, Jr. *Red Earth, White Lies: Native Americans and the Myth of Scientific Fact*. New York: Scribner, 1995.

George-Kanentiio, Doug. *Iroquois Culture and Commentary*. Santa Fe, NM: Clear Light, 2000.

Graymont, Barbara. *The Iroquois in the American Revolution*. Syracuse, NY: Syracuse Univ. Press, 1972.

Hauptman, Laurence M. *The Iroquois Struggle for Survival: World War II to Red Power*. Syracuse, NY: Syracuse Univ. Press, 1986.

Hauptman, Laurence M. *Conspiracy of Interests: Iroquois Dispossession and the Rise of New York State*. Syracuse, NY: Syracuse Univ. Press, 1999.

Jemison, Peter G., ed. *Treaty of Canandaigua 1974: 200 Years of Treaty Relations between the Iroquois Confederacy and the United States*. Santa Fe, NM: Clear Light, 2000.

Jennings, Francis, ed. *The History and Culture of Iroquois Diplomacy: An Interdisciplinary Guide to the Treaties of the Six Nations and Their League*. Syracuse, NY: Syracuse Univ. Press, 1985.

Johansen, Bruce E. *Life and Death in Mohawk Country*. Golden, CO: North American, 1993.

Mattheissen, Peter. *Indian Country*. New York: Viking, 1979.

Porter, Robert Odawi, ed. *Sovereignty, Colonialism and the Indigenous Nations*. Durham, NC: Carolina Academic, 2005.

Porterfield, Kay Marie, ed. *Encyclopedia of American Indian Contributions to the World: 15,000 Years of Inventions and Innovations*. New York: Facts on File, 2002.

Richter, Daniel K. *The Ordeal of the Longhouse: The Peoples of the Iroquois League in the Era of European Colonization.* Chapel Hill, NC: Univ. of North Carolina Press, 1992.

Shattuck, George C. *The Oneida Land Claims: A Legal History.* Syracuse, NY: Syracuse Univ. Press, 1991.

Shenandoah-Tekalibwa, Joanne, and Douglas M. George-Kanentiio. *Skywoman: Legends of the Iroquois.* Santa Fe, NM: Clear Light, 1996.

Snow, Dean R. *The Iroquois.* Cambridge, MA: Blackwell, 1994.

Tehanetorens. *Legends of the Iroquois.* Summertown, TN: Book Publishing Co., 1998.

Tehanetorens. *Roots of the Iroquois.* Summertown, TN: Native Voices, 2000.

Wallace, Anthony F. C. *The Death and Rebirth of the Seneca.* New York: Knopf, 1970.

Wallace, Paul A. W. *The White Roots of Peace.* Philadelphia: Univ. of Pennsylvania Press, 1946.

Weatherford, Jack. *Indian Givers: How the Indians of the Americas Transformed the World.* New York: Crow, 1988.

Wilson, Edmund. *Apologies to the Iroquois.* New York: Octagon, 1978.

Zinn, Howard. *A People's History of the United States.* New York: Harper and Row, 1980.

Index

About the Authour

DOUGLAS M.GEORGE-KANENTIIO was born and raised on the shores of the Kaniatarowanenneh (St. Lawrence) River on the Akwesasne Mohawk Territory. An award-winning writer and journalist, he has served the Mohawk Nation in numerous capacities, including as a land claims negotiator, a co-founder of Radio CKON, and the editor of the news journal *Akwesasne Notes*. He is the author of the books *Iroquois Culture and Commentary* and *Skywoman: Tales of the Iroquois*. From 1996 to 2002, he was a member of the Board of Trustees for the National Museum of the American Indian. He once had the honor of bearing the Olympic torch. He resides on Oneida Territory with his wife, the singer Joanne Shenandoah.